From Junkie to Joy

My Miracle Can Be Yours

Konrad Strawn
Deena Reed

1st edition 2025

Contents

Acknowledgements

Louise Allen, without your promotion of Konrad's success story at Marshall Community Center this book project would never have even been thought of.

Clark County Talk, the article you published about Konrad's success story inspired by the poster Louise created was a catalyst for this book.

Apryl Mar, thank you for creating the amazing book cover! Your input was divine.

Brandon Margicin and Mike Olson, thank you for the interview and all the kind words.

Roxann, your input and efforts to get this project going is much appreciated.

Jesse Reed, thank you for sharing your incredible spiritual experience as well as your unwavering support for the time it took to complete this book.

Matt Rud and the Punchy Books Accelerator course, if you want to write a book and don't know how to get started, I recommend this fantastic team of professionals.

Aidan Strawn, for your willingness to share your perspective. Your input is raw and honest. Thank you.

Our test readers, Bob, Brady, Deana and Marsha thank you for the editing and feedback.

Tammy Bryan, if you had not told Konrad that he should write a book this project would not have happened. That suggestion changed our lives and hopefully many more.

Thank you to all of our friends, family and associates that encouraged us along the way on the writing process of this book

Introduction

Joy is possible even through devastating, heart wrenching insurmountable sadness and depression or catastrophic events. This is Konrad's story of heart wrenching, life changing circumstances, and choices. He is a great example of never giving up. I want to start by explaining how this book is written. Konrad wrote a lot but because of aphasia, a language disability from the stroke, he isn't able to actually write this book. I, as his mother, am acting as the editor/author of his inspiring story. We have had some touching and healing moments as we work through this project together. Neither one of us really remembers the pain and suffering his self destructive choices caused. The pain of having your children addicted to heroin is a good thing to block out. Konrad's stroke erased most of his memory.

An old friend of mine reached out to me because she found Konrad on Facebook. Her son has been missing for five months. He also fell into the lure of drugs and is still struggling off and on as many addicts do. Could he have gone up in the woods and will never be seen again? This absolutely wrecked me. Where is the joy in that? I cried out to God for some time during church one morning, weeping, and then I suddenly shifted my thoughts to feeling grateful that God put my old friend and I together again, and I began to feel delight and joy bubble up deep inside me and I knew my perspective changed for writing this book. God prepares us for everything and puts the right people in our life to bring comfort. I experienced a migraine for two days after reading her "missing person" posts on Facebook, but the joy of seeing her again overpowered the worry and fear before we actually got together for lunch. God is awesome.

God is the author of JOY. We have to hang onto it and literally fight for it. So before Konrad tells his story, I feel it's important to give you a few working definitions.

Junkie: Disparaging and offensive, a person who is addicted to narcotics, especially to heroin.

Joy: The true definition of joy goes beyond the limited explanation presented in a dictionary: "A feeling of great pleasure and happiness." True joy is limitless, life defining, a transformative reservoir waiting to be tapped into. It requires the utmost surrender and, like love, is a choice to be made.

Miracle: Supernatural phenomenon, a highly improbable or extraordinary event, development, or accomplishment that brings very welcome consequences. A surprising and welcome event that is not explicable by nature or scientific laws and is therefore considered to be the work of a divine agency.

Konrad says "I am a miracle. There must be a destiny."

I am pretty sure that around 2007 there may have been a parent or two who would have liked to kill him for what he led their kids into. I know I wasn't thinking too kindly towards the ones that introduced Konrad to those drugs. We are told that about ten to twenty of those friends are not alive now because of drug use. Konrad says that they were just sick without their drugs and not really friends. My heart goes out to the suffering alcoholics and addicts as well as their families. The struggle is real and I can barely see through the tears as I write this, seventeen years later.

There is inspiration in Konrad's story for stroke victims and their families as well as suffering addicts and alcoholics. A big part of this story is about recovering from a massive brain hemorrhage caused by an Arteriovenous Malformation (AVM). Thank you all for joining us on this healing journey. May you be encouraged and find hope as we share how God strengthened us through our families' awe inspiring experiences.

1

I Was Born A Normal Kid

I was born a normal kid. My sister and I were raised in Woodland, Washington where we lived as a family from 1990 until 2007. My dad lived there until 2012 when the house was finally sold after being on the market for four years. My mom moved in with her parents in July of 2007. My parents divorced in January of 2008. I was kicked out around February of 2007 during my senior year of high school because I was eighteen, and had stopped going to school. Instead of focusing on graduating from high school all I could think about is when and where my next fix was going to come from. My drug addiction was so bad at that time I was completely numb while my parents were going through a divorce.

I was a very active kid. I only stopped moving when my mom read books to me, or when I started reading books to her. I have always loved to read books. My sister Roxann didn't like to read with us as much. When she was a toddler, she would walk by and knock the book out of my mom's hands. Later we discovered that she needed glasses, so reading was less enjoyable for her. She loves to read now.

When I was learning to read my mom's parents lived in Idaho. On Spring break of 1st grade I read all my Dr. Seuss books over and over on the way to visit them. Good thing I kept all those Dr. Seuss books to help me relearn to read all over again after my stroke.

My grandparents didn't live in Idaho very long because of health issues. Grandpa Burk had 2 large strokes and 3 small ones. Grandma Burk had Ovarian Cancer. While she was going through radiation treatment my grandpa had the first major stroke. His strokes were ischemic. This type of stroke is caused by a blockage that prevents blood flow from getting to where it is supposed to go. The type of stroke I had is called a hemorrhagic stroke. This is when brain tissue is damaged from direct contact with blood. My grandparents had to move back to Washington to have better access to their health insurance. Our trips to Idaho to visit them were a lot of fun. At Christmas time there was a lot of snow so we got to go sledding on their property.

We always had cats and kittens. Our tom cat George, who lived the longest of any cat we had in Woodland, loved to eat squirrels. When I was six, I said, "Squirrel guts to George are like popsicles to me." I loved popsicles! We also had many other cats. Apparently, I was kinda mean to them or my sister whenever I was hungry, tired, sick, or anxious about some report, band concert or anything else. We lived on a very busy road, and if the cars didn't run over the cats, the coyotes got them. On one occasion a cute little fluffy gray kitten was injured getting away from a big bird.

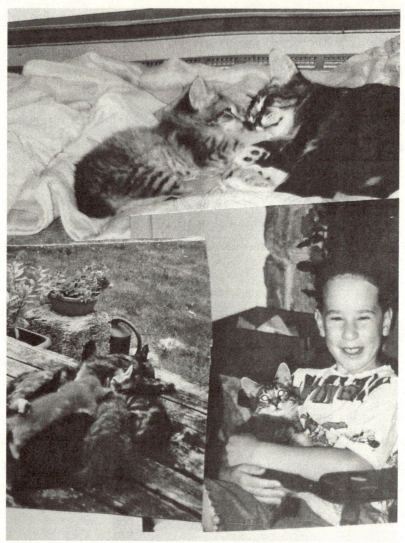

Konrad With Our Cats

When I was seven years old I got a new bicycle that my dad tried out in our field. He ended up damaging his kidney when he crashed my bike, and had to have it removed. Good thing my parents weren't drinkers now that he only had one kidney! That was a stressful time. My mom started working at La Center school and my sister was going to school as a kindergartner.

We raised pigs and one day my mom forgot to turn off the water, and they were slipping and sliding in the mud and squealing when they hit the electric fence. There were huge puddles in the whole pen. On the day we butchered one batch of pigs, we had some friends come over to watch. My mom brought out some homemade cinnamon rolls and no one was even interested in eating them. Not a very appetizing combination.

Raising Pigs

Speaking of drinking, we did go to a lot of parties. My dad's friends were a close knit clan that got together a lot. For example, there was an annual camping trip at our friend's cabin on the North Fork of the Lewis River Road, up by Moulton Falls. It was great playing in the river. One year I fell against a rock and broke my pinky finger, but all in all those annual camping trips were a lot of fun.

My sister Roxann and I played soccer from eight years old through middle school. My mom coached both of our teams. Our teams were always good because she worked us so hard at practices. For a couple of years my team had an advantage because we had two orphan boys from Liberia that were very talented. One year our 9/10 year old co-ed team was so good that we had to play the 11-14 year olds. We never won any games after that, but we sure had fun trying!

Roxann and I also got to work at the Ridgefield Refuge the summer between 8th and 9th grade. She is 2 years younger than me. Unfortunately, she followed in my footsteps quite a lot. With that first job I spent the money I earned and bought a car. My grandpa Strawn had fixed up a nice red four-door Chrysler sedan that my parents helped me buy. Eventually, I wrecked that car and every car I had after that. I had three cars in the six years that I could drive. I lost my driving privileges when I was 22, then I had a stroke at age 23. The Stroke left me too disabled to ever drive again. My bicycle and parents are my main forms of transportation now.

I loved playing my Game Boy so much when we drove anywhere in my early teens that I didn't pay any attention to how we got where we were going. So you can imagine I had a hard time finding my way around when I started driving. No fancy cell phones back then. My parents gave me a road map!

So basically I had a pretty normal childhood. Even though we lived in Woodland, we went to La Center School located in La Center, Washington, 12 miles away from our house since my mom worked in La Center. She worked at a restaurant where she met my dad until the restaurant closed. She then got a job at the La Center School. My daycare lady lived in La Center too.

In high school I especially enjoyed track and cross country. My coach, Mr. Holmes, was also the high school principal. Mr. Holmes had high hopes for me as an athlete on his cross country team. At the 2004/2005 end of season celebration, Mr. Holmes presented me with an award for most improved athlete. He was very disappointed when I began using drugs and getting into trouble. This poor choice of mine was heartbreaking for Mr. Holmes as well as many others that had watched me grow up in this small school district.

I started experimenting with drugs fairly heavily around the age of 16, after starting to work as a busboy at the Oak Tree Restaurant in Woodland. Marijuana was the first drug I used. At times I still think about using marijuana. I went to many parties and tried all kinds of drugs and cigarettes: alcohol of course, cocaine, crack, meth, and then I tried heroin. That ended up being my nemesis. I loved it and hated it, mainly I hated the sickness I experienced from withdrawing.

In my junior year I began a program called "Running Start" that allowed me to get college credits while in high school. I was doing really great at that time. However, I had too much free time and started going down the wrong path when I started hanging out with kids who didn't go to school at all in the afternoons. College in the morning, and partying with high school dropouts in the afternoon was a *sure* recipe for disaster. One of those friends died of an overdose a few years later.

In addition, I was a really good student and was able to get a very high score on the WASL (required state testing) even while I was high on drugs. At this point, Mr. Holmes had no choice other than to ask me to leave La Center High School and transfer to Woodland High School. He said that I was a "cancer" in our school with my drug related behaviors. I was on a boundary exception to go to La Center so he invited me to go to my home school because I had a lot of influence with my peers. He also said that I should have all my freedoms taken away from me, and only have a desk and bed in my room at home. No more jobs, cars or friends. As I also had suicidal tendencies at this time, my mom thought that punishing me that severely would lead to me killing myself. I felt ugly because of acne on my upper arms and even my birthmark bothered me. I caused a lot of unrest, pain, disappointment and suffering for my family.

Konrad's 2006 Senior Picture Woodland, Washington

In general, the addiction of a loved one is frustrating, heart wrenching, exhausting and leads to bouts of anger, hysteria, sadness and deep depression. Depression that makes it hard to get out of bed from paralyzing fear and despair. Fear of finding their loved one dead from an overdose, or worry about them being killed in an accident. Parents, *please* don't blame yourselves, unless of course you stuck the needle in their arm. It's not your fault. Addiction is a spiritual disease. The enemy is demonic, ugly, baffling, powerful and cunning.

After being asked to leave La Center High School, I began attending Woodland High School where I was enrolled in an alternative program which is probably why I aced the GED test four years later in July of 2011, when I was 22 years old. That program focused on preparing students for that I guess. I was excited to enroll in college after passing the GED test.

I remember the first time I used heroin with a needle. I was at my friend's house and the euphoria from using a syringe was so great, I soon became so dependent that my body was in pain without it! The pain is like nothing you can imagine, like you are going to die. I became so sick, spiritually, emotionally, mentally, and mostly physically. Life became all about preventing and relieving that unbearable pain crawling up my back. Using it was such a relief. It was like being thirsty for water. I had to have it or become violently ill. That is *all* I cared about.

When my girlfriend Cindy got pregnant with Aidan, I finally had something in life to live for. We were only 18 and 16 years old at the time but I would probably not be alive today if Aidan had not been born. Aidan says that it wasn't fair to bring him into the world when we weren't able to take care of a child. Fred, Cindy's father, suggested that she should have an abortion. But Cindy's Step-Grandpa Ron, who raised her, was in full support of us taking on the responsibility of having a baby. Including having us live with him. Cindy's grandpa still helps out today, seventeen years later. Fortunately or unfortunately, I really don't remember very much about my childhood before the stroke. But memories are coming back, slowly but surely, as new connections are formed as my brain continues to heal. With the encouragement of my family and my determination I have come a long way since then. God's mercy took the worst memories from me of when I was suffering from this addiction.

As I previously said, after leaving La Center High School, I started going to the high school in Woodland where we lived. But soon, I was not going to any school at all, as I dropped out soon after Christmas vacation in my senior year just before turning 18. My dad convinced my mom to stay together until I graduated from high school. Well, I was 18 and not going to school anymore, so my mom kicked me out of the house as she was sick of my lying and manipulating. I thought I was so clever in hiding my addiction. But when they began watching me nod off while sitting in a chair and sweating when I was "high" (always wearing long sleeve shirts even in the summer), they started to realize that something was very wrong. To say the least, my erratic behavior as well as the blood splatters all over my bedroom wall, and scattered syringe caps in my bedroom, and other places around the property, caused them a great deal of distress. I simply could not be without heroin. I was so sick it felt like I was going to die until the relief came through that needle again. I would puke before going into work as a busboy at the Oak Tree Restaurant, and apparently my mom found a pile of vomit next to my car one day. I was excited to finally begin training to be a server. Being successful at work and maintaining my drug habit was too challenging. That job at the Oak Tree lasted about 3 years.

After I was kicked out of the house by my mom, I lived with my girlfriend Cindy at her

step-Grandpa's house in La Center. She was two years younger than me, and became pregnant with Aidan around her 16th birthday in March of 2007, very soon after I moved in. My son Aidan became the only thing I lived for. I now had a purpose and a desire to live. I was so sick of fighting the pain and chasing the relief that I finally asked for help after Aidan was born.

Aidan was born in November 2007, and shortly after that I finally entered an in-patient treatment program at Portland Adventist Hospital in Portland, Oregon. When I went into treatment, Cindy and I were planning to get married and raise our son together. My mom took me to my first treatment program. Once again, I was acting very bad. I had an abscess on my foot from using needles and was so "high" at the time, that I told my mom it was a spider bite. On our way to the treatment center we had to go to an urgent care clinic because I could hardly walk. So she had to use a wheelchair to get me into the urgent care clinic. My mom was so mad and humiliated! I was at Portland Adventist Hospital for in-patient treatment in January of 2008. I turned 19 during my stay there.

While at Portland Adventist I learned that only about 7% of heroin addicts can overcome the terrific PAW's, also known as Post Acute Withdrawals that last about 18 months. Symptoms of PAW's include restless legs and the crawling feeling that makes it hard to sleep. This is what weakens the will of people to stay off opioids. But my mom believed in me, and told me that I could become a successfully recovered addict. She thought if I could easily be in the top 10% of my class in grades, I could stop using heroin too.

By the time I got out of treatment in late February 2008, Cindy had decided that another guy was Aidan's father, because she thought Aidan looked like him and wanted him to do the paternity test instead of me. I was devastated over the news because I wanted to marry Cindy and become a family. Of course, this led to a breakup and eventually I relapsed into using heroin again. But Cindy's father, Fred, was very generous with her and Aidan. He bought her all kinds of baby items like a car seat, crib, diapers, and clothes. Fred even bought Cindy things too, including a nice new winter coat. All this even though he had never believed that she was his daughter. So Fred and I "crashed" the paternity test appointment so we could all get tested. Fred wanted to know once and for all whether or not he was Cindy's father and I, of course, wanted to know if I was Aidan's father. This was a big mistake as you can only imagine how awkward that was. Come to find out, we had to have paperwork done which takes about 3 weeks to process. I don't know if Fred ever did a paternity test or not, but his mom, Grandma Carol, has always been a big part of Cindy's life as well as Aidan's. She adores Aidan just like my grandma did.

The question of paternity set me back tremendously, but I was still willing to be Aidan's father and take complete responsibility, either way. So I moved into my grandma and grandpa Burk's house with Aidan because my mom was living there at the time. My sister Roxann stayed out in Woodland with our dad because she was so mad at my mom for leaving. Nana, my mom's mom, was so loving, and took such good care of Aidan and me. I will never forget the way she took care of us. She and my grandpa lived for their family. Grandma Carol was a big help too, as Cindy and Aidan stayed with Grandma Carol a lot. Nana is my Grandma Burk, my mom's mom, and Grandma Carol is Fred's mom, and Cindy's grandma. Those great grandmas were so helpful. I don't know what we would've done without them. Grandma Carol gave us this picture she took of Aidan enjoying a fudgesicle for the first time. I love the joy that shows on his face as he is experiencing this special treat. I hope it makes you smile too!

Aidan eating his first fudgesicle

During the time I lived with my grandparents I was on methadone. Methadone is an analgesic drug that is similar to morphine in its effects, but lasts longer and is used as a substitute drug in the treatment of morphine and heroin addiction. Like other prescription medications there is no plan to ever stop using methadone once you begin using it. It takes a very strong determined person to stop using methadone. All opiates are opioids, but not all opioids are opiates. The two terms can be used interchangeably. Natural opiates are derived directly from the opium poppy, like morphine and codeine. Semi-synthetic opioids are created in a lab by chemically altering natural opiates. Heroin is in this category and is made from morphine. Synthetic opioids are entirely man-made in labs and not derived from the poppy plant. Fentanyl and methadone are examples of synthetic opioids. Methadone is sometimes used for severe pain when other medicines don't work. However, there is some risk in using methadone to overcome heroin addiction because you can still use opioids, therefore making it easier to overdose.

I had to get up and get to the clinic to get my methadone before 11 am every morning. Missing one dose would bring on the incredible sickness from withdrawals. This clinic was only about a mile away and it was stressful for my family when it looked like I wasn't going to make it in time to get my dose of methadone. Fortunately, living at my grandparent's house made it easier to get to the methadone clinic. In my journal, I talk about being clean and sober for 50 days, and about being so sad that Cindy had cheated on me. My journal has prayers to God. I am not sure exactly why I stopped going to the Methadone clinic, possibly because I owed $380. Most likely it was because I started using heroin again. I was going to ask my dad for the money, but once again, I'm not sure what happened during that time. Post acute withdrawal symptoms last for up to a year and a half, and not having the methadone was just another form of withdrawal. Despite my early relationship with Jesus, I relapsed yet again and resumed my heroin use. My journal also speaks of long days of loneliness and boredom. I just don't remember the details of this relapse.

After my treatment at Portland Adventist Hospital, I went back to work at the Oak Tree Restaurant. I don't know how long that lasted until I relapsed and lost my job. I applied for unemployment but I did not do my job searches as required, so I was denied any more unemployment. So then I applied for TANF (Temporary Assistance for Needy Families), sometime in 2008/2009, so I could take care of my Aidan and myself. TANF helps with food and cash.

While I was still clean and sober, my mom took me to many Alcoholics Anonymous meetings. I met a man named Jesse at one of the meetings that was close to my grandparent's house, which I could walk to. Jesse has a huge heart for single dads because he was a single dad that raised his daughter since she was a toddler. Jesse could not have custody of his daughter without the help of his mom. He was still living with his mom until after he married my mom. I was so very fortunate that he took me under his wing. He would take me to lunch after the meetings and displayed so much compassion for my situation of being a single father of an infant. He, too, knew what it was like to have a small child who depended on him. One day at an AA meeting, I was able to introduce Jesse and his buddy to my mom. He was very experienced in the ways of addiction and my sister Roxann and I couldn't hide anything from her ever again!

There was an AA speaker meeting that featured live music that I wanted to go to. It just happened to be on the same night as the Al-Anon speaker meeting that my mom had planned to attend. (Al-Anon is a twelve step program for the loved ones affected by those suffering from addiction and alcoholism.) But I was able to convince my mom to go with me to the AA meeting instead. However, I canceled on her at the last minute in order to go to work, but my mom still wanted to go. She loved the spiritual aspect of the AA meetings and was always welcomed warmly. Some churches are very welcoming in this way also. Church and 12 step programs are designed for people to walk through life's challenges in community. God did not design us to be alone. Keep searching until you find a church that is welcoming and gives you a sense of belonging. Anyway, my mom suggested that maybe Jesse or Rod could take her. Well, Jesse agreed to take her to this speaker meeting with live music. My mom thought it would be awkward to go to an AA function by herself, since she wasn't an alcoholic. Even though Jesse ended up having the flu, "something" told him to go anyway. This of course impressed my mom. During the evening she realized that he considered it a date and not just a ride, and the rest is history. They have been married since Christmas of 2010. I got to be the best man!

After a year or two in 2009, Roxann wanted to move in with all of us at Grandma and Grandpa Burk's house. That was great, except I couldn't share a room with her, so Grandpa said that I had to move out because I was a man and my sister was a girl. So Aidan and I moved into an apartment in Hazel Dell with a friend named Chris. We lived next door to a girl named Nikki who had a brother named Jeremy that stayed with Nikki often. He had a girlfriend and kids, but apparently his addiction made it difficult to live harmoniously with anyone. We all became good friends and did a lot of drugs together. Jeremy's sons and my son grew up and got caught up in using drugs. Very sadly, two of Jeremy's sons died from overdosing on drugs. Aidan got hooked on Fentanyl in high school and almost died several times. He was surprised to wake up alive many times. Aidan said that withdrawing from fentanyl was the most traumatic thing he has ever experienced. Thank God Aidan survived those years of abusing drugs.

At this time, Roxann and I became closer than ever. Any childhood struggles were behind us, and we became very close. She came over a lot and played with Aidan. We had a lot of fun hanging out together. Roxann thought our couch was terribly ugly, but Chris and I were very proud of that couch. My behavior was rather ugly at that time too. My son says that I would tie him to that ugly couch so I could do my drugs in another room. (His mom told him that.) And things got very bad from there.

Chris eventually moved on and Jesse's friend Steve moved in with Aidan and me. Steve is the friend that helped Jesse raise his daughter Jessica. He always brought donuts to her because she wouldn't eat much else. Steve was also a great help in taking care of my son.

After losing my job at the Oak Tree Restaurant in Woodland, I decided to apply for financial assistance so I could afford to take care of Aidan. But in order to do this, I had to take a paternity test. I was so nervous and anxious about it because I had put off the test for more than a year and wasn't sure what the test results would reveal. Finally, on January 20, 2009, I found out that there was a 99.9% chance that Aidan was, in fact, my son! At the time of getting the test results, Aidan was almost fifteen months old. To say the least, I was so happy and relieved to know the truth at last.

Back to that ugly couch, we unfortunately let a very bad man stay with us in the apartment and sleep on that couch. I was terrified of this guy. We all were. Although my memory simply cannot recall what happened exactly, my sister said that he swindled me and threatened me into doing bad things. Like using more drugs, selling drugs, writing fake checks, stealing checks, etc. He even had my car stolen. For example, I got caught stealing food from a local grocery store, and was charged with a misdemeanor. I was asked to not go back to the store for 100 years. The check forgery led to a felony charge. I was later able to get that felony vacated, which was key in getting a job a few years after the stroke.

We got my car back after it had been stolen, and then I wrecked it in Longview, Washington, and got in trouble for driving under the influence of drugs. My dad bailed my "dumb ass" (his words) out of Cowlitz County Jail again. Then he told me to get clean, or tell my son Aidan goodbye forever. My dad has paid for so many of my mistakes. This was my third attempt at getting clean. The second treatment was after getting a felony from forging checks. He bailed me out that time too. He loves his family so much. After that, I began a deferral program, and went to detox at Sunnybrook Hospital. That was when I started using Suboxone, to make it possible to quit using heroin. Suboxone is buprenorphine/naloxone. This medication blocks the "Opioid Effect", unlike methadone, which you can still use opioids with. Suboxone makes you very sick if you use opioids with it. Suboxone shrinks the receptors in the brain, unlike methadone, which stretches the receptors. I was so afraid of running out of Suboxone that I would save 2 out of the 3 pills per day that were prescribed to me, just in case I didn't have Kaiser insurance anymore. My dad had to get rid of over 900 pills after I was free of all of it.

Before I got into treatment again, I ended up in the hospital with a huge infection on my right shoulder from using syringes. I have quite a scar to remind me how bad things were. After I got out of the last treatment, Aidan and I moved in with my dad at the house in Woodland. I called Aidan "Mini Me". I was teaching him new words like nocturnal. He was four years old then. Now that he is older, that word means even more. Maybe I taught him that word because he didn't sleep well at night. Looking back, he has had a lot of problems going to sleep at night.

Not getting enough good sleep could be part of his own struggles with life, school, etc. We used to go on long walks every day. There is nothing quite like the energy of a healthy four year old. I love my son more than anyone or anything. God is first but that is different.

2
My Path to Faith, Hope and Love

All was going very well. I started going to a NA (Narcotics Anonymous) meeting in Woodland. I soon became the chairperson of that meeting. We met once a week on Friday evenings. These meetings were mandatory for two years. I was a natural at leading the meetings. The kids in school always wanted to be in my group because I always knew all the answers. Also, my dad drove me to Longview twice a week for mandatory counseling. I got my GED when I was 22, the summer before my stroke. The pre-test was easy, and then I aced the GED exam. The people were amazed at my grade on the actual test without even studying. I was getting ready to enroll in college. My grandpa Strawn was going to pay for all of it, as well as for any one of us that wanted to go to college.

It was through going to the NA and AA meetings that my sister and I learned that if we wanted to be free of addiction that we had to completely surrender our will to a higher power. Drugs have an evil power and only God can free you. Jesse and my mom started going to church in June 2011, about 4 months after I got clean and sober. Jesse had gotten a DUI in January of 2011 so he had a new clean and sober date as well. As a result of his DUI, he went through a treatment program to ensure he didn't lose his driver's license. So in June 2011, Mom and Jesse invited me to go to church with them. So being curious about this Jesus/God thing, I went.

There was an Alpha course that my mom, step sister Jessica, sister Roxann, her boyfriend and I all attended. The meetings were held at the YMCA in the community room where we were going to church. The YMCA gym is transformed into a sanctuary every Sunday morning. The Alpha course is an informal program with videos and books to answer all the questions you may have about the Christian faith and what it means to follow Jesus. It was a great time of learning, praying and eating delicious food provided by this lovely lady named Eka. She was an amazing Christian woman. I learned so much. There was even a beach retreat weekend in Tillamook, Oregon where we could learn all about the Holy Spirit. I opted not to go to that but Jesse, Roxann, Jessica, my mom and Roxann's boyfriend went. They all had a wonderful time. Jesse was working a swing shift at that time so he didn't join us for the Alpha course, but did attend the Holy Spirit weekend where they learned a lot about the Holy Spirit.

John 14:6 is a very powerful scripture. Jesus said to him, "I am the way, and the truth, and the life. No one comes to the Father except through me." Learning about Jesus and the Holy Spirit changed everything. I got in the habit of reading my bible every day and journaling. Now I do that on Sunday mornings because I do so much exercising the rest of the week. The first journal entry when I started reading the Bible is pretty funny.

9/29/11 Genesis 1:1-23 So begins a 365 Day Plan to read this big-ass book!

After that Jesse, Roxann, my mom and I started taking an INSTE class at the home of one of the church leaders whose name is Triston. INSTE is a bible college that is taught by an instructor in a home setting. This was a college level course entitled, "A Walk Through the New Testament". Everything was going really well. I loved praying during the class. Even Triston said that I put him to shame with the eloquence of words that poured out of me. I really wanted to continue on this path and was scheduled to go on a mission trip with my Grandpa Strawn the summer of 2012. I loved doing my homework and just like school was able to memorize scriptures easily and get the meaning of them with little effort. On Sunday's we would meet my sister before class and I would quickly help her get caught up with her homework. I would've aced that class if I hadn't had a stroke. Roxann didn't pass the final exam and neither did Jesse. My mom was able to get a high grade even under the circumstances of what was to become a devastating, life altering event.

3

A Bomb Hiding in the Shadows

As part of my deferral program, I had to do counseling and attend meetings. My favorite meeting was in Woodland called "No Matter What". I love the name of that meeting. I continued to stay sober and do my jail duties such as community service, and stayed at my mom and Jesse's apartment while I did my community service in Vancouver Washington, about 45 minutes south of where I was living in Woodland.

I was very excited about that special day which fell on Friday, February 24, 2012. I was going to celebrate my one year "clean and sober" date at the meeting with my cherished friends who were staying clean and sober with me. We were planning to celebrate with cake and much love! But all my friends were surprised when I failed to show up for the meeting, especially since I was the regular chairperson of that meeting. That evening I didn't know that the next time I would see my friends would be when they visited me in a hospital under extreme circumstances. They didn't know if they would ever see me again after that, it looked very grim and shocking to anyone who came to visit me. I had experienced overdoses before and was glad to be revived sometimes, and not glad other times. This was different. This was a hemorrhagic stroke. This was a ruptured arteriovenous malformation. (AVM)

I was hanging out at home with Aidan that fateful day. We can only piece together what happened exactly, partly because of another stroke survivor's story. A book called "My Stroke of Insight" by Dr. Jill Bolte Taylor. She was a Harvard trained Neuroanatomist who has studied the brain a lot. She had an AVM in the same area of the brain as I did. An arteriovenous malformation is where the veins are directly connected to the arteries instead of being buffered by the capillaries. She was able to determine that she was having a stroke and was barely able to use the phone before she didn't know what the phone was even for. This helped us understand why I didn't call 911 or my dad for help.

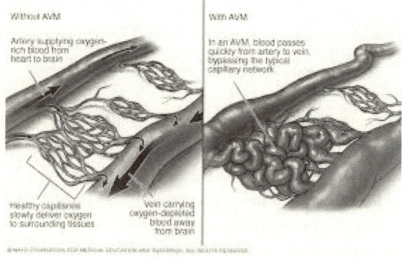

Picture of an AVM

Now is where so many miracles began to happen. My sister called about 1:30 pm that Friday afternoon to congratulate me on one year clean and sober. If my dad had not changed his mind about doing his errands after work I would not have a story to tell. He had a feeling that he should go straight home. When he got home he found me moaning and all curled up on my bed with some frozen peas and corn on the headboard. I guess I had a headache when Roxann called and she suggested I put something cold on my head. My wrists were all bent which is a sign of brain damage. The chair by the phone was knocked over as well as the table and the lamp. I was probably trying to get to the phone to call 911 and just couldn't do it. How terrified my four year old son must've been that day.

My dad first thought that I had used again and was overdosing or something. He called 911 and when the paramedics came they could not find a vein to put in an IV because I had ruined all the accessible veins. I had even used the veins on my penis as is common for junkies. The paramedics tried eight times and then finally put the IV in the shin bone. They drove me to Legacy Hospital in Salmon Creek instead of PeaceHealth Medical Center, where I was supposed to go as a Kaiser member, because they didn't think I would make it that far.

One of the responses to the book progress posted on Facebook was nothing short of miraculous. It turns out that the daughter of a very close family friend saw the ambulance coming down the Lewis River road and began to pray for the person in the ambulance and their family as she was driving up the road that day. Perhaps that was the second miracle that day. Maybe that was the reason the paramedics decided to take me to Legacy Hospital instead of PeaceHealth. Prayers are so powerful. That was the first of many prayers that went up for me and my family. If you ever get the urge to pray, just do it!

Of course my dad went to PeaceHealth Medical Center and was very surprised and upset that I was not there, so that was incredibly stressful. When my parents both got to Legacy Hospital, as well as Roxann, Dr. Le said we needed to decide whether we wanted to do anything. Because if I survived I may not like being in a wheelchair unable to talk, walk or even see. My mom was full of faith and told the doctor to get in there and fix me right now! My dad wanted to call his dad and ask him what they should do. Grandpa Strawn said to trust God. Konrad will still be alive. Dr. Le said that he could not fix the AVM because if he tried it would just cause more bleeding. He could only go in and open up the skull and let off the pressure from the swelling. Then later the doctors could go in and fix the AVM by going in through the arteries in the groin. My parents agreed to try to save my life. Dr. Le went into surgery and five hours later came out and said "I got it. I got it all. The veins cooperated." Absolute answer to prayer. My mom's faith never wavered, she knew that Dr. Le was going to fix my brain.

This is my CT scan. The dark and the bright spots show the parts that were damaged.

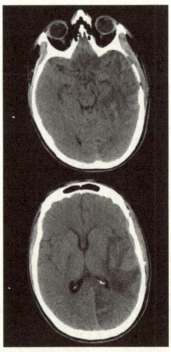

*Konrad's CT scan after his
stroke*

It was a miracle that I was still alive. 12% to 66.7% of people that have an AVM hemorrhage in their brain drop dead immediately. The rate of long term disability is from 30% to 50%. One percent of the country has this bomb in hiding. Anyone can be born with an AVM. It is usually discovered in people ages 20 to 40. Some of the symptoms include: sudden severe headache, nausea and vomiting, weakness or numbness on one side of the body, vision changes, speech difficulties, seizures, and loss of consciousness. Treatments include surgery to block the vessels, an Embolization, (this is where a catheter is inserted through an artery in the groin or wrist and it is moved to the location of the AVM, and then a glue-like substance is released to stop or slow the blood flow through the AVM.) This is generally used when there is a large malformation with a lot of bleeding. This can reduce the chance of a rupture. The doctor said that I was born with a missing capillary that led to the vein and artery being directly connected, and it could have ruptured at any time. What are the chances it would happen on this very special date?

One year clean and sober, how could that be a coincidence? I believe God has a destiny for me. Do you believe in coincidences? My cousin Mike died five years later on February 24, 2017 from an overdose.

- February 24, 2011: I got clean and sober

- February 24, 2012: I had a massive brain hemorrhage caused by an AVM

- February 24, 2017: My cousin Mike died from an overdose

What could God's plan for my life be? He is clearly not done with me. Why am I still alive?

4

Miraculous Healing Journey Told by My Mom Deena Reed

As Jesse and I walked into that hospital on the day of the stroke we were brought into a room where I saw my daughter wailing. She had lost her best friend forever. Even if he survived he would never be the same. That hardly phased me at the time. Her wailing phased me of course but I was not fearing for my son's life. God gifted me with incredible faith in that moment. I had made the mistake of praying to God for something really big to strengthen my faith. Konrad had been praying that Aidan's mom could see him more. God has quite a sense of humor. Prayers need to be specific. If you pray for patience you will experience many opportunities to practice patience.

Cindy and her boyfriend took Aidan home with them that night from the hospital and he didn't live with us again for two years. This was a pretty rough time for Aidan. They really struggled to take care of him and their new baby that was born one day after Aidan turned 5.

When I got to see Konrad he was laying in a bed with a light sheet over the lower half of his body. I kept covering him up saying that he doesn't like to be cold. No one told me that the brain damage fried his internal thermostat and that he would not want to be covered up with blankets. That would've been very helpful to know.

As we were leaving Legacy, a nurse was remembering when he was brought in and how his pupils were triangles. That meant that the brain damage was severe. I could've gone *without* knowing that little piece of information.

After Konrad had gone into surgery, I immediately called Triston, the leader of our INSTE class and asked him to come pray with us. He came as well as bringing Konrad's spiritual partner from the class. Triston, David, Jesse and I prayed. Triston prayed for God to spare him because he has evangelism in his soul. God is clearly not done with Konrad. This brought some peace and comfort. They left and we went on waiting for Konrad to get out of surgery. When Dr. Le came out with the surgery report, I was delighted, but not surprised at all.

The next day Dr. Le had to put in a drain tube for the cerebrospinal fluid because of the swelling. It could be in for ten days and then we would have to put in a shunt if it didn't stop draining.

The pastor of our church came and prayed for him as well as the pastor that we did a weekly Bible study with. Everyone that we knew said they would have their church pray. There were probably a hundred or more people praying for our family. We were all lifted up so much. One morning very soon after the stroke during our church service, that lovely woman, Eka, got up in front of the congregation and prophesied that Konrad was going to be alright. I wasn't quite sure what "alright" meant but that was very encouraging to everyone that was there. Everyone knew Konrad and had been praying.

I had one bad day, but otherwise I was confident of a full recovery. It was the day the doctor took him off the heavy sedatives. I had forgotten that he was on Suboxone and would be withdrawing. The male nurse that day just followed the doctor's orders. The Doctor said he had a strong heart and could handle it. Well, it was a long day of Konrad's heart racing and him panting. I cried on the way home that day wondering if we had done the right thing by saving his life. The next morning his dad reminded the doctor that he needed his Suboxone. He was withdrawing from Suboxone. Then his uncomfortable day of heart racing and panting all made sense. Luckily they make it in strips that go under the tongue. They gave him his Suboxone and then he slept peacefully that whole day. I was so relieved. Konrad later said that they should have just let him detox off it so he did not have to remember the pain of withdrawal. He later chose to get off it and tapered it down properly. That was very difficult and he had a lot of sleep disturbances.

Our family had to decide what the long term plan was going to be. He had a breathing tube down his throat and a feeding tube down his nose. We were in a large room with a lot of family. Konrad's grandpa Strawn, his wife Donna and cousin Carolyn and her husband Harold were there to help us decide what the next steps were going to be. Konrad's cousin Lish had come to visit from out of town. Lish's dad, Uncle Gerry and his wife Denise were there. My parents were there. Roxann was there. About thirteen people in all. Someone had brought in a therapy dog and they said that the dog would go to the ones that needed the most comforting. I was surprised at where the dog went. The dog came to Jesse and I first and then it went over to Konrad's Grandpa's cousin Carolyn. Anyway we decided to put in a tracheostomy and a feeding tube directly in the stomach. Konrad says "I have a lot of scars from Legacy Hospital."

Lish was one of the most memorable visitors at Legacy Hospital. This was within the first few days of the stroke. She was leaving the room and glanced back and saw their Grandma Strawn standing behind his bed. She died in 1985 from a car accident. Lish was about six years old when that happened so she knew her grandma. An awesome moment. That very night Konrad's dad had a dream of his mom and Konrad walking down a path in a grassy field together.

Konrad liked classical music so it was constantly playing in the background while he was recovering. I had to convince the staff that not only does it help the brain heal but he actually likes it. He plays it constantly to this day. He likes jazz music too. He plays it at such a low volume that I can hardly hear it. Acute hearing is another result of his brain damage caused by the stroke. Over the years he has had to go to urgent care a few times to get the wax washed out of his ears from wearing ear plugs all the time. His ears are not quite as sensitive now. He uses a fan at night because for years he went to bed at 7:30 pm and the rest of the house was still watching TV or making noise of some kind. Weird routines like getting up at 3:30 am in the morning and eating the same exact things every day is another aftereffect of the stroke. We have finally convinced him to go to bed later and get up later so the rest of us can sleep. He has a better schedule now and goes to bed at 8:30 pm and gets up at 4:30 am.

Jesse's daughter Jessica was learning to drive while Konrad was in the hospital in intensive care. I was very thankful for that time with her, otherwise she would have felt pretty left out. We were pretty preoccupied, with most of our time spent at the hospital. As parents, teaching a kid to drive is a very special time in our lives. There is not very much opportunity for that kind of quality time together once they have their license and independence. It keeps them away from home more and more until they move out and start their own lives.

He had another very special visitor from grandpa Strawn's church that came twice and laid hands on him and prayed for him. Sam was known as the angel of death because he was the one that always made the hospital visits. The first time he prayed, about ten days after the event he opened his eyes. I can still see that day clearly in my mind. The room was bright and Pastor Sam was at the bottom of the bed. Amazing! A week later he came back to pray again. I wasn't there that time, but Konrad's dad said that the hair on the back of his neck stood up and when he opened his eyes this time, it was like someone was at home.

So of course, on the very last day that the drain tube for the cerebrospinal spinal fluid could be left in, it stopped draining and the doctors were able to remove that without having to put in a shunt. That was a relief. I was very grateful and delighted, and down deep I was not surprised.

His very first PT, (physical therapy) session consisted of him getting out of bed and sitting in a chair. He couldn't hold up his head so they tied a strap around his head to a chair so his head didn't flop over. After seventeen days in the ICU it was time to move him upstairs to a regular room. But that didn't happen because they decided that moving him upstairs and then moving him again to a convalescent center would be too disruptive. So it was time to move him to Fort Vancouver Convalescent Center. (FVCC)

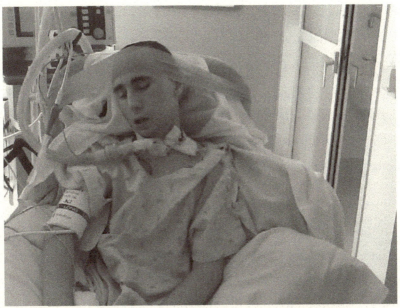

Konrad's first physical therapy session after stroke

As we were getting ready to leave the hospital I asked Dr. Le what the prognosis was. He looked at me and motioned to his computer and said that what was going on in that room did not match what the CT scans were saying. He said that he was clearly not the one in charge here. He said it would take about two years for recovery. So of course I imagined him being completely back to normal in two years. Well, normal includes Homonymo Hemianopia. (HH) This is where Konrad is blind on the right side of both eyes caused by the brain swelling. The eye nerves are in the back of the skull and were damaged from all the swelling. He only sees half of your face when he looks at you. It could be more severe where a person can only see the food on half of the plate. His OT, (occupational therapist) said he was able to compensate very well. He has a significant limp from spasticity. There is very significant stiffness in his right ankle also known as drop foot or foot drop. He has done extensive physical therapy for this and it has resolved some. He wears a brace at work for safety. No amount of

Physical therapy, exercise, massage or leg braces seem to be able to resolve the limp. He has spasticity in his right hand as well. He is unbelievably determined. He uses his right hand for everything as much as possible. When he is in a hurry he will resort to using his left hand. Aphasia is also a significant deficit from the stroke. The damage from the blood directly on the brain tissue was in the language part of his brain. He had to relearn language all over again.

We met a guy named Ian that had an AVM in the middle part of his brain and he could communicate very well. His limp was pretty significant and he said that he wished he had done the exercises more right after his stroke. He was pretty sad and depressed. He was with a girl that he met in the hospital during physical therapy and she had her AVM fixed before it caused much damage. She was having headaches and her doctor was very wise to do a scan because her neck and shoulder muscles did not seem to indicate normal tension headaches. She only had to do a little physical therapy for a short time. It was an interesting visit. It was nice to have two other young people that had had AVM's come to our house to encourage Konrad.

5

Next Step, Fort Vancouver Convalescent Center

They convinced us that the tracheostomy had to be in for at least three months before it could be removed, to minimize scarring. Later on we talked to the doctor that put it in and he said that he could put it in on Wednesday and remove it on Friday if he wanted to. It seemed that the only thing it got used for was to clear out the yucky flem from his lungs. This went on for far too many days. Watching the staff clear his lungs was awful. They did not have experience with tracheostomies. It appeared that there was an infection in his lungs.

One of my favorite memories while he was at FVCC was when he removed his own tracheostomy shortly after he started to talk. His first words were, "I love you." He said some other weird stuff but I don't remember what it was. Everyone kept pushing on it to cover up the hole so we could understand him. After about two days of this, I got a call at four o'clock in the morning asking me to come to the emergency room because Konrad pulled out his tracheostomy and they were going to put it back in. Thank God I got there just in time to stop them from doing that. He leaned over, looked at me and said, "Thank you!!! You are the light!" They returned him to the Convalescent Center. He saw his speech therapist the next day and she said, "You didn't need that thing anyway did you." Then she gave him some pudding. I honestly thought that we were going to have an appointment with an Ear, Nose and Throat (ENT) doctor that week but they had actually pushed that appointment out two weeks. I was lucky I was able to convince them not to put that thing back in.

Learning to communicate again was a tremendous undertaking. He knew nothing. Just the other day he called his lip his cheek. He had to relearn everything! They told us not to say a word more than three times because he would get frustrated. The only ones that got frustrated was us after saying it ten plus times until he could finally pronounce the word right. Then he wanted another word to pronounce. This went on forever. He was relentless. His dad said a trip to Clackamas to see doctors was excruciating because we had to constantly come up with words for him to say all the way there and all the way back. He had to learn every part of his body again which at times, I think we didn't quite get all of them taught. Eyebrow was a tricky one.

My mom was the most amazing woman in the world. This journey would've been a lot harder without her support. While he was at FVCC she came every day and would move his arms around to the point that he got full range of motion in his arms. Not only that but she would make him stick out his tongue over and over and purse his lips into a kiss. If he wasn't so smart he may not have picked up on these physical cues of all of us kissing at him and sticking our tongues out at him. I was working with his legs because I was a little stronger and I am a Licensed Massage Therapist. I have spent countless hours trying to relieve the spasticity in his right leg. I don't feel too bad though, his PT that he has been working with for the last two years couldn't make any changes in that leg either. The leg and the blindness is why he rides a bike everywhere instead of driving a car.

Here is a picture of his favorite visitor at the convalescence center.

Aidan's visit with his dad at Fort Vancouver Convalescence Center

Konrad gained strength pretty fast. After about six weeks at FVCC he was ready for the next step. RIO, Rehabilitation Institute of Oregon.

6

RIO At Good Sam Hospital

One of the first things the staff at RIO did was to cover one eye because he was seeing double. That was amazing. He seemed more comfortable after that. PT included a lot of eye exercises. Eventually he saw an eye specialist that got him into a pair of glasses to help with the double vision. She was a very skilled eye doctor. She gave him some stickers to put on the lenses to mimic Peli Prism lenses. These would help him catch a glimpse of anything in his right peripheral. The purpose was to train his eyes to look in that direction after catching a glimpse of something. He hated them but wouldn't take them off. If they were helpful they could be put into the lenses of his glasses permanently. After one month with the stickers on his lenses, we went back to see the eye doctor and she tested his eyes again and he didn't have to wear any glasses at all anymore. That seemed like a miracle. In just one month he learned to compensate for the Homonymous Hemianopia. (HH) Recently he said that he could only see half of my face when he looked at me. I finally understood what it meant when they said he compensates well.

The other task that RIO had was to get him to be able to shower and dress himself. He was very strong and obsessive about doing the strengthening exercises. They wanted him to use a cane. He didn't really want to. So he managed to get strong enough to walk without the cane. Konrad tossed the cane into the garbage and said he was done with it. He probably should have continued to use it anyway. That is what the professionals recommended. He uses one now because of the hip fracture and his limp is not as drastic while he uses the cane.

They made him a leg brace for the foot drop. He did not like that either. He gained some weight and then it was so uncomfortable that he wouldn't use it anymore. Maybe if he had continued using a brace and the cane his limp wouldn't be quite so bad. He had some vertigo and nausea that the staff had some great tricks for too. Because of the right side's weakness I always walked on his right side which probably helped him compensate for not being able to see on that side. He had to always look for me or anyone else that was on his right side. We had to walk closely with him at all times for quite a while. He loved to walk and walk and walk so this was a big commitment for his family to always be by his side.

Soon they had him ready to go home. He needed to be somewhere that he had twenty four hour care. This is one of my favorite miracles. Jesse and I were living in a two bedroom apartment on the second floor with his daughter. We couldn't afford anything bigger at the time we moved into the apartment. My daughter Roxann had to stay behind at grandma and grandpa's house. That was very upsetting. Our lease was up and we did not sign another lease at the apartment so when we needed to get a larger place we were free to do so. We found an angel from a management company that found us a daylight basement house that accepted pets and was big enough for all of us. It was only a three bedroom house. We were moving into that house the weekend that they wanted to send Konrad home. I took a leave of absence from my job to take care of him. Fortunately, I had enough sick leave to take a year off work to take care of my son. Surprisingly, the house was not very clean as you would expect, moving into a rental that was managed by a rental company.

My daughter hired our friend Tina and she came and cleaned our house while we were all moving our stuff in. She taught Konrad and Cindy how to vacuum and to clean their home when they lived in Cindy's grandpa's mobile home. Tina and I helped clean Ron and Cindy's house, when Konrad lived there after Konrad got kicked out. Cindy's grandma had passed away a few years prior and nothing had been touched since. We thoroughly cleaned the mobile home and taught the kids how to keep it up. They had no garbage service so it took a couple trips to the dump to empty the living room. Tina was a blessing that day as well as the day she helped us get our house ready to move into. She was a professional house cleaner, not just a close friend. Roxann managed to get part of the deposit back which was a blessing because we didn't have enough money to make the move without it. It worked out perfectly. Roxann was so much help with her brother and nephew. Konrad is very blessed to have such a strong supportive family

7

Konrad Is Home, Now What?

Now comes the acute phase of therapy. Weekly PT, OT and Speech Therapy kept us very busy. We got lots of great exercises to do to improve balance that I did with Konrad back and forth across the small living room. Besides eating and sleeping this is pretty much all we did for about a year. When we weren't exercising we were taking walks and saying words so Konrad could gain back his ability to communicate. Konrad, Roxann and I would walk around the neighborhood and at each mailbox we would stop and tell Konrad what it was and he would repeat it. Then we would go to the next mailbox and ask him what it was and he didn't know. There was also a beautiful three mile trail a few blocks from our house. I would sing the "Zip a Dee Doo Dah" song to him as we walked along and he loved that. An airplane in the sky was a complete blank look of confusion. This was the routine for months. Here we are at the rental house, me, Konrad and Aidan.

Deena, Konrad and Aidan at rental house after stroke

We had a couple of checkups with Kaiser's Neurosurgeon. That surgeon just went on and on about what good, well thought out and planned work Dr. Le had done. He said that he wished he could claim that work as his own. The next time we went to see him a month later he said again that he wished he could claim that work. I was silently wishing that Konrad would be able to have more language at this point. It was really nice to hear that the surgery Konrad had on his brain was so good, especially since Dr. Le said he was only going to open the skull to relieve pressure from the swelling. The progress was slow and discouraging at times. I am absolutely certain it would have been a lot worse if we weren't covered with the powerful prayers of so many people.

In July 2012, we had our first social worker visit. This is a two to three hour intake on Konrad's caregiving needs. The most amazing thing in this visit was when she asked Konrad if he was suicidal. He actually understood her and emphatically said NO! Another surprise to me was when she told him that he could live in a group home with other people that had disabilities if he wanted to. He said. "No, I want to live here with these people." At that time he had no concept of mom or even son but he loved us and knew he wanted to be with his family. He mixed up "he" and "she" for quite awhile. The social worker said a few things that I was a little bit in denial of. While we were talking with her he got up and went to the kitchen and started eating some fruit. Watermelon probably, we ate a lot of watermelon that summer. She said that was a "thing" or result of the stroke. He couldn't sit any longer and wanted to go for a walk so he started walking back and forth across the street without us. She said that too was a result of the stroke and not just him wanting to get stronger. Lastly he loved everyone and wanted to hug them. She cautioned me about that too. Someone could take advantage of him. I, of course, thought to myself. "Well he is never going to be alone. I will be with him." That was very unrealistic. She authorized ninety one hours a month of caregiving to be paid by the state. This was for someone that required twenty four hours a day supervision. I had to take some classes to become his caregiver. He could not even walk up the stairs without someone by his side. Thank God for a supportive family.

During the care-giving classes I met a woman who was caring for her daughter. She had brain damage from encephalitis. There was a severe infection in the front part of her brain that disabled her. That is when I saw a stark difference in how we were handling our devastating event with prayer and what it looked like without prayer. There was little to no joy in her family's healing journey.

Three bedrooms upstairs for the kids. Konrad, Roxann and Jessica. Jesse and I were in the daylight basement. This wonderful house had a very small living room and a one-butt kitchen where you could not even have the dishwasher and refrigerator open at the same time. On the weekends Konrad went to stay with his dad and Aidan came to stay with us, to give us and Aidan's mom a break. When Konrad discovered this, he refused to go to his dad's unless Aidan came with him. His dad said it was like taking care of two four year olds. It took Konrad until November of that year around Aidan's 5th birthday to remember his son's name. Aidan came to stay with us for about a week when his baby sister was born. He shared his dad's bed as usual. He didn't like to sleep alone. He was quite a wiggly kid to sleep with. He had slept with Jesse and I many times. Aidan's little sister was born on November 16th, one day after Aidan turned five. It took nine months for Konrad to finally remember his son's name. Aidan got to share a room with his daddy again, if only for a week.

One weekend when his dad brought them home he was exhausted from reading Clarence the Clown. He said, "It took three hours to get through that book. I never want to see that book again." I completely understood how he felt. We spent many hours reading Dr. Seuss books so he could learn to talk and read again. It took two hours to get through an alphabet book, "Big A Little a." No matter how many times we read that book he did not pick up on the pattern but he never got frustrated or tired of reading the books. Roxann enjoyed helping him so much that she said that she wanted to become a speech therapist.

On November 25th, 2012, Konrad started writing in his journal again, his first journal entry after the stroke:

11/25/12 The Bible in Pictures For Little Eyes – Who, who, who. I just wish I could do everything.

God, thank you. I am still trying to listen. Let's just try. Thank you!

Roxann made a journal entry in his journal that day. She probably helped him write all that. Her entry: I am very happy to have my brother around still. He may not be perfect yet, but I love him and know he will be back to perfect very very VERY soon!

I love you God, thank you for everything and thank you for my brother's progress and continued progress. And thank you for the love and support from my family for me and my amazing brother! I love you. Amen

Konrad used to read the bible every day and journal about what was going on and what it meant to him in his life. He started reading "The Bible in Pictures For Little Eyes" when he started journaling after the stroke. Eventually he graduated to his normal bible.

Julie, his speech therapist, was such a lovely lady and a highlight of our week. We enjoyed going to see her the most. She had another patient that had very similar speech problems so she invited them to have some sessions together. The other patient was an older lady and apparently had brain cancer. She had purchased this $300.00 aphasia workbook that she left with Julie when she died. Julie passed it on to Konrad. That was an unbelievable gift. Most of it has been too hard to do, all the grammar stuff is still very challenging. Konrad has just recently started to work in that book again. I have been pleasantly surprised at what he has come up with. And a little bit sad at what he still can't do. He has figured out that he can cheat by using his phone, or look at the answers in the back of the book. Putting mixed up sentences that he has to put in order is still too challenging, so he has his phone tell him the right order for the words in the sentence.

When we saw his occupational therapist he was surprised at what the social worker said about his eating. He was convinced that he was thin and since he didn't sleep a lot like many brain injury patients do, he just needed more calories. Well, he went from 128 lbs. to 174 lbs. He was starting to look uncomfortable. Then one day my mom, Nana, suggested that he eat salads. When he tried that, he lost two pounds in a day or so and now, for lunch every day he eats a big bowl of veggies with a protein and an avocado. He eats many servings of fruit daily too. No sugar or processed foods. He's back to about 128 lbs again, and has kept it there for the most part. The part of his brain that tells him that he is full is broken along with that internal thermostat. It is pure discipline or perhaps the routine the experts said he would need that keeps his diet so much the same every day. They told us he would need routine and quiet because his hearing was magnified. He listens to the radio non stop at a level I can barely hear. He wore ear plugs for many years to soften the noise level. We were told not to have more than one conversation going at one time. Jesse is hard of hearing so you can imagine the problem that creates. My hearing is not as good as it used to be either. We like the TV louder. Good thing Konrad is getting less sensitive these days. They told us to keep talking to him because that would help him get his language back. His dad calls him every day just to talk to him for a while.

Thankfully he is so full of love and gratitude that it has made this journey of healing joyful. Many brain injury patients are very cranky about their situation even to the point of not wanting to live. Konrad is an inspiration and we are all blessed with his great attitude.

8

Divine Encounter

This is my favorite story of a divine encounter while out and about with Konrad. We had been to a therapy appointment and decided to stop for lunch. Taco Bell in Orchards. I really wanted to just go through the drive through because Konrad could not read the menu anyway, and I didn't know what to order for him. I just wanted to get food and go to the post office and then home.

In my car, I had a book ready to mail to my cousin who was interested in knowing more about Jesus. Her friend had just become a christian so she was curious and asking questions, and she knew we had recently started going to church. The book was called "Heaven is for Real" by Todd Burpo. It's a story about a four year old boy that had an appendicitis attack and almost died. He went to Heaven where he met Jesus and his sister that he didn't know about from a miscarriage. The reason I was so compelled to give her this book was because of the way the boy was so distressed and adamant that to get to Heaven you had to know Jesus.

So everywhere they went in their travels they would see pictures of Jesus and his dad would always ask him if that was Jesus. Finally he saw a painting called "Prince of Peace" by Akiane Kramarik. She was eight years old when she painted it. She had been having dreams and visions since she was four years old and she was finally inspired to paint Jesus. The boy said, "That's

him. That's Jesus." There was a picture of "The Prince Of Peace" in this
book.

Prince of Peace by Akiane Kramarik

Well, my husband had a vision during worship at church shortly after we
started going to church in June of 2011 that is very similar to many near
death experiences. In this vision Jesse was at the foot of the cross and he

could hear the noise and smell the smells from all the people that were at the crucifixion of Jesus. He felt overwhelmed by the mood of extreme sorrow and pain. There was the wailing coming from the women. He smelled the stench of death, the suffering was massive. The sky was darkened and the ground was muddy and sticky as Jesse dropped to his knees and began sobbing. Perhaps the ground was wet from Jesus' blood. He saw the name plate they put on his cross above his head. The Bible tells us that it said, "King of the Jews".

All of a sudden Jesse was in another realm. In this part of the vision he was walking down a beautiful path in a vast field of tall grass. He stretched out his arms and the grass, some kind of grain, was softly touching his fingers. He was in awe with the sweet fragrance of flowers. Possibly lavender, honeysuckle and many more. It was as bright as the noonday sun would be, except that there was not a sun in the sky. It was wonderfully warm, about 75 degrees. The grass was waving as if there was a slight breeze but there didn't seem to be any wind. He turned to the left and there was Jesus! His eyes were piercing as he looked at him, and it seemed as if it cut clear through him with an unimaginable love. Jesus' indescribable, unconditional love. He had instant recognition, an absolute knowing that it was Jesus. He was beautiful with straight brown hair and a Mediterranean complexion. Jesus assured him that he would have climbed up there on that cross even if it was only for him. He was loved by Jesus. Jesse was full of trepidation and fear. He was filled with a phenomenal love. The message that was communicated was just, "I am, I am the One you seek." The love encompassed peace and Shalom which is more than just peace. It is peace, love, joy, mercy, grace, authority and prosperity in all things. Jesus loves us so much and forgives us from past present and future sins. Because of that LOVE, kindness, mercy and grace that we cannot quite fathom, we love Jesus, and follow Him by loving others and putting God the Father above all else. Just saying that Jesus loves you can sound so contrite but it is so deep that it is beyond our comprehension. Being a recovered addict himself it was easy for Jesse to think that Jesus died for everyone else but not for someone like him. When he came out of the vision he was on his knees and struggled to stand back up.

As I was interviewing Jesse about this incredible experience he was wracked with Godly sorrow about how he has been behaving the last five or six years. Jesse started using marajuana in 2018 to help with pain. Well, when you are a recovered addict you cannot just use something like that. It goes straight to abuse and addiction. It has come to a head during the writing of this book. That chaos has finally come to an end. About four years ago he got laid off from work and the resentment and hate started to build up into physical distress. He is still suffering some physical issues that are bringing him to his knees and closer to God than ever before. God has reminded him to count his blessings, and that He has given him everything, his wife, family, skilled hands to be productive and a beautiful home for us all. God has given us opportunities to bless others that need help. So why be so bitter? Jesse has been greatly humbled once again.

When I was about to package up this book to mail it to my cousin, he flipped through it and said, "That's Jesus. That's who I saw in the vision." Of course, now I did not want to give away this book because it had a picture of Jesus in it. But I decided to send it to my cousin anyway. The book was in the car ready to mail when we had a divine encounter at Taco Bell.

So, here we were at Taco Bell and Konrad insisted that we go in and eat. I finally agreed. He still had very little language at this point. We were standing in line and this lady came in behind us, probably an angel. I motioned for her to go ahead of us because I had no idea what to order. We ordered our food and went to the drink station and got some drinks. We sat down at a table next to the drink station. I looked over and saw that lady, we will call her Sue, and she was praying over her lunch. I thought that was awesome. I'm not sure how the conversation started but we were talking to her and I told her about my dilemma with the book I was about to mail to my cousin. She pulled out a wallet size picture of "The Prince of Peace" from her purse. She gave it to me and told us where we could buy more. Of course I felt somewhat silly then. Konrad scooped up that picture and put it in his wallet and it is still there today, thirteen years later. She said that she almost sat where we were sitting but "something" told her to move over one seat. As she was leaving Konrad called out, "I love you!" She replied, "I received that." What a powerful moment. Then, as we were leaving, he looked at me and was like, see, he couldn't express in words but he made it clear that we could've missed that encounter if we had not gone in to eat. Not long after that we went into a Wendy's and he was hoping for something like that to happen again but nothing unusual or interesting happened. I think he was a little disappointed.

9

Seizures

Our family liked to get together quite often, about once a month for a game night, with lots of food and fun. My favorite part was playing pinnacle with my uncle and parents. We haven't gotten together for a game night since before Covid. My dad passed away in October of 2019 and my mom died in October of 2021. This particular game night on Saturday August 4, 2012, was at my brother's house in Battle Ground. Aidan was having so much fun playing with my brother's kids. His cousins Luke and Troy weren't very much older than he was and they had a blast. We did not leave until about midnight. In hindsight I wonder if keeping Konrad up so late and all the lights on our way home had anything to do with the seizure he had the next morning. He was always one to have to go to bed early, around eight o'clock, or he would not feel well the next day. We were getting ready to go to church the next morning when I heard a big thud from upstairs. I ran upstairs and Konrad was on the ground convulsing terribly. The doctors had wanted him to take anti-seizure medication but he refused. I called 911 and learned that cell phones could tell the dispatch where we are. I was told only landlines could do that. Anyway, that little four year old that had eaten an unusually big breakfast vomited all over the floor when he saw the ambulance take his daddy away again. Typically, Aidan wasn't a big eater in the morning, my heart broke for that little boy. Konrad came home from the hospital later in the afternoon and was just a little bit tired. I can't imagine what it must've been like for Aidan.

This led to regular doctor appointments with a neurologist. The neurologist convinced Konrad to take some anti-seizure medication. He started out with the minimum dose. About a year later he was at Marshall Community Center and he had another seizure. Pretty dramatic for the folks at Marshall Community Center, because he was pretty well known there. He did not get a CT scan after this seizure because they didn't think he should have one at this time because he had already had so many. He was one CT scan away from having the maximum amount anyone should have in their lifetime. His anti-seizure medication dose was increased again. Then, about a year after that he had another seizure at Marshall Community Center. His dose has been at maximum ever since. Konrad's dad read an article in a newspaper about hemp helping people reduce the frequency and severity of seizures, so Konrad has been eating organic hemp hearts every morning since then and has not had a seizure since. It could also be that his brain has just healed enough to not have seizures anymore. Now he takes his medication every twelve hours and eats hemp hearts every morning to prevent any more seizures.

10

Effects of Trauma

Anyone curious how all this has affected Konrad's son overall? Aidan has been such a blessing, but it has not been easy for him. Quite the contrary actually. Well, about the time my kids were eighteen and sixteen I would make the comment that grandkids are the reward for not killing your own kids. I was also wondering about that time, why was it that I even wanted to have kids in the first place. I wanted this? What was I thinking!!! Teenagers are so hard, especially when they are doing self destructive behaviors. Family is of course the greatest blessing of all, no matter how difficult it can be. Not long after I mentioned that grandkids were a reward for not killing your own kids, Konrad announced that his girlfriend was pregnant. Children are a gift from God. This turn of events is what saved Konrad's life. Being addicted to opioids is no way to live. Jails, prisons, institutions and death are the outcomes of this painful lifestyle. Konrad now had a reason to live. At that time I had no idea that I would get to help raise Konrad's son Aidan. Aidan was deeply loved by all his family, especially the great grandmas. When Konrad and Aidan lived with my parents, my mom was absolutely delighted. Great Grandma Carol is Cindy's grandma on her dad's side and she was madly in love with Aidan too. She helped Cindy a lot and took tons of pictures of him. Cindy stayed with Grandma Carol often then, so Aidan spent a lot of time with them as well as with my parents. This was when Aidan was an infant.

Aidan lived with Konrad while he was living in an apartment. Then Konrad and Aidan lived with Konrad's dad in Woodland after Konrad got into trouble with the law. Konrad's dad helped Konrad and Aidan a lot. It seems like many grandparents help out with raising kids in Aidan's generation.

Konrad's dad is teaching Aidan to drive now, taking full responsibility for getting him to driver's ed and making sure he has enough hours of practice driving.

Aidan slept with his dad until he was four years old. Konrad just showed me a book that his cousin Lish gave him. That funny book confirmed my memories that Aidan has always been a night owl or "nocturnal" as Aidan informed me when he was three. The book is called "Go the Fock to Sleep." Quite hilarious as you might imagine with a title like that. Apparently, it is also quite common for kids that have ADHD to have trouble sleeping. He was diagnosed with ADHD in elementary school. As he got older more diagnoses were given. The most recent is CPTSD. Complex Post Traumatic Stress Disorder. This is caused by experiencing many traumatic events or abuse in childhood. Aidan's birth was a little rough too. He was over seven pounds and a few weeks early. Aidan and his mom stayed in the hospital for 5 days and he lost a little weight. Almost two pounds.

On the day that Konrad had his stroke Aidan was four years old. He was alone at the house with his dad that day. According to Aidan, in the afternoon he told Aidan that he was going to go out to get firewood because we had a wood stove. He stumbled into the house and down the hallway from the garage. When he got to the living room where Aidan was playing his Leap Frog game, he went to the front window facing the driveway and main road. Konrad was looking out the window and holding his palm over his eye in pain. He was groaning in a low pitch tone. The phone started ringing and ringing. It was very scary to Aidan. Konrad started across the living room and knocked over the table and chair going to the phone. The chair is an heirloom in a pink color with soft fabric and a high back. The arms of the chair were hand carved. Konrad tried to grab the phone and fell over the chair backwards. He was screaming bloody murder with pain, screaming for help. Konrad made his way to get frozen peas and corn for his head to ease the pain and then made his way to the bedroom. On the way he ran into the door at the end of the hallway. It was extremely loud.

Aidan just dictated the memory of this tragic event to me in a way that I had never heard before. Now he needs a break. Big terrifying memories that caused him to start shaking.

The night of the stroke Cindy and Jake came to the hospital to take Aidan home with them not knowing if Konrad would ever be able to take care of his son again or even survive the brain hemorrhage. Aidan went home with his mom and he didn't get to see his daddy for weeks. Aidan went to the hospital that fateful day with grandpa and went home with his mom and Jake. It was so precious when he finally got to visit his dad in the hospital.

Aidan's mom and Jake had to do the hardest part of a child's early years. Aidan had to start sleeping alone in his own bed. He lived there with his mom and Jake until he was six and in first grade. They really struggled to get him to kindergarten with a brand new baby to care for. He missed a lot of kindergarten. In First grade he was still missing school a lot, then Cindy and Jake broke up so Aidan got to come and live with us and his dad. Aunt Jessica had just moved out so he got to have his own room.

He has been living with us since then, except for half of his sophomore year when wasn't going to classes at school. I texted his mom asking her if she had a place for him to stay if he continued not following our rules. That was a Friday, she promptly came and got him that night saying that she and Konrad had already talked about this six months ago. He stayed with his mom for the rest of his sophomore year except for any night that wasn't a school night. Weekends and any night that wasn't a school night he stayed with us.

Cindy took him to his old school on Monday because she had things to do and thought we would be mad if he missed school while she was getting him transferred to Ridgefield High School. Then, he got kicked out of school that day when he and his friends overdosed and almost died. Two of them went to the hospital. Aidan called Jesse to come get him. He ended up walking home. There was at least one other friend involved. Aidan tells us that he was addicted to fentanyl and tried to kill himself many times with it but kept waking up. He said the withdrawal from quitting fentanyl was the worst trauma he had ever experienced. Benadryl was a nasty trip but he kept doing it. We would constantly find new packages in his bedroom.

He was doing much better at Ridgefield High School with his mom's help. He really wanted to be at home where all of his friends were. He has matured so much in the last year. Aidan has been through so much counseling that he counsels his friends. He is very empathetic and caring towards his friends. Many of them have experienced adversity during their childhoods too. Aidan is working very hard to get through High School and get prepared to be a successful contributing human being. He has had to do a fair amount of advocating for himself to get the kind of support he needs to be successful. Kids that have experienced a lot of trauma have a high stress window. It does not take very much stress to get them dysregulated. Emotional dysregulation can be caused by:

- Genetic factors

- Early childhood trauma

- Chronic invalidation of emotions

- Poor modeling of emotion regulation by caregivers

- Traumatic brain injury

- Mental disorders

Dysregulation looks like fight, flight or freeze. Zoning out is another response to stressful situations, almost like certain kinds of seizures. When you ask a kid to read, and that kid gets upset and crawls under the table you know that they are done, or dysregulated until they can calm down. When Aidan was in sixth grade during Covid, I got to help him with his school work that was all online. We were almost done with a math assignment one day when he started to roll around all over the couches. I could not get him to finish the last three problems. He had become dysregulated. These behaviors are very frustrating and confusing for the ones who are trying to get a kid to do something normal people would not think twice about, like closing his dresser drawers. Clutter is also a problem for people that have experienced a lot of trauma. Completing tasks seems to be an issue too. These are a few of the battles we have struggled with over the years.

I work at an elementary school so I have had a bit of training. I couldn't understand why Aidan was always with the counselors in elementary school instead of just in class doing his work. Now I understand. There seems to be more and more kids with dysregulation issues each year. Aidan has been fortunate to have worked with many skilled counselors to teach him how to manage those big emotions. Trying to educate the rest of our household is *very* challenging. Jesse, especially, just thinks he needs more discipline.

All of us have had a fair amount of trauma and can be very reactive instead of understanding. His family not acknowledging, or even knowing how much progress he has made in the last year does not feel very good to him. When his dad freaked out because he missed a day of school, is a great example of us being triggered by previous times of him missing school and the worry, stress and fear that it caused us. It triggered terror in my heart when I heard he skipped out for a day recently because of all the school he missed his sophomore year, and the dangerous things he was doing while not in class. He thought we were overreacting because he is doing so much better and we just didn't see his progress. Thankfully we had a great conversation after that and I felt reassured that he was making great gains. He is genuinely remorseful for causing anyone else pain and stress. Sometimes we can be harder on ourselves than anyone else is.

Aidan is working with the counselors at his High School to overcome some of the problems that he has caused for himself with self destructive behaviors. He has tried different medications in the past to treat ADHD and depression. He has gotten the most relief from meditation. He has been trying to get me to meditate. There is a counselor at his school that is from LifeLine Connections that is going to work with him using hypnosis. As of July of 2025 he started taking Buspirone for the overwhelming anxiety. This drug is generally prescribed for people over 18. I guess his doctor thought he was close enough. So far, it has helped more than any other medication we have tried over the years. He doesn't want to use it forever, so hopefully this will get him through his senior year.

Mental health is a very prevalent problem in our society. My hope is that a lot more resources get allocated toward mental health issues in the coming years. Not just for the children but for the homeless people, veterans and anyone else with mental illness that is struggling to live a normal life.

11

BIRC, Brain Injury Rehabilitation Center

About a year after the stroke Konrad was blessed with the next phase of rehabilitation. All of the physical therapy, occupational therapy and speech therapy for the acute phase was over. Yet he was a LONG way from perfect as his sister would say. The acute phase of therapy was stopped after about six months. He got to go to BIRC for a total of eight weeks about a year after the stroke. This was a life changing opportunity. The people at BIRC are very knowledgeable at what they do. The last few weeks were stretched out with less days per week. One thing they tried to get him to do was to tell people when he didn't understand. They wrote it down in his journal/planner. What we all didn't know was that he did not know what "understand" meant.

The first thing they did was get him hooked up with C-VAN. C-VAN is C-TRAN's paratransit service that is an origin to destination shared ride service. They take people that can't drive to places with a reservation at least 24 hours in advance. This service is weather permitting with the exception of things like dialysis appointments. The rides are all within Clark County, Washington. C-VAN gave him a ten year pass. After that he reapplied and got the pass renewed. The people at C-VAN are pretty smart, they did not allow me to go with him for the assessment. They came to the house and picked him up and took him to the Transit station to interview him.

This way I could not do the talking for him as I was accustomed to doing. Konrad got a ride to Oregon's Paratransit station from his cousin Mike, the one that overdosed in 2017. Trimet gave him a three month temporary pass so he could ride the bus to BIRC. One of his family members would take him across the bridge to the Transit station near Jantzen Beach. Riding the bus was a major step to independence. It took a lot longer to get places with the bus compared to having someone drive him, but it was very important to get him used to riding the bus.

Konrad spent six hours a day at BIRC doing various types of therapy. Speech therapy was one of the major parts of his day. He was doing Occupational therapy one day and while he was trying to open a can using a regular can opener, he sliced his hand open. I got a call to come get him and take him to urgent care for stitches. He had never used a can opener like that growing up. I had one that took the lid off without any sharp edges. Konrad was not supposed to get it wet for twenty four hours. The next morning he was going to wash his hands and I told him not to do that. "Go dry your hand off." I told him. He went right to the sink and turned the water on. This happens still today, you think he understands something when he really doesn't. An instruction like, it's on top of the refrigerator, would totally confuse him. It took quite a while for him to relearn the name of all his body parts as well. There are probably still some today that he doesn't know.

The most exciting part of BIRC was the physical therapy. He had two therapists, Chris and Ruth. Chris even came to our house and picked Konrad up and took him to a nearby gym. Marshall Community Center has been a huge part of Konrad's life ever since. Chris took pictures of all the equipment and marked out the ones that he was not to use, and taught him how to use all the other ones. They made several trips to Marshall

Community Center to teach him how to use the gym. He had a notebook full of pictures. Ruth gave him pictures of different stretches to do. She told him that stretching was very important for the human body. This was the beginning of a beautiful thing. Marshall Community Center has been a big part of Konrad's life since he was first introduced by his physical therapists from BIRC.

Before Konrad got a job he would get his son ready for school each morning, walk him to school, and then get a ride on a C-VAN and spend the day at Marshall Community Center. There he would take swimming classes, fitness classes, work out on the equipment and eat lunch while talking to all the people that would talk to him. In the beginning, during the summer after his therapy at BIRC, I would go with him and take swimming classes with him. One day I realized that all that swimming had worn out my swimsuit and it had become very thin on the back side. That was kind of embarrassing, and I promptly got a new swimsuit. Konrad continued this routine of going to Marshall Community Center every weekday that he wasn't at the Val Ogden Center trying to get a job. It took four years to find a job.

Konrad wanted to interview the front desk customer service person, Brandon, from Marshall Community Center that he had gotten close to. After a few weeks of asking Brandon to call us so that we could interview him about Konrad and his inspiring and positive presence at Marshall Community Center, he finally called. Brandon has helped Konrad every year renew his membership or temporarily cancel it while he was busy volunteering for the Summer Meals Program to help feed the hungry kids that depend on school lunches as their primary source of food. Konrad has been doing this for eleven years. He has Mondays and Fridays off from his job now and he and his dad go and volunteer on those days for the Summer Meals program. It fills his heart with joy.

Brandon had nothing but positive things to say:

- Everybody loves Konrad.

- His perseverance and positivity is inspiring to other members and guests.

- He talks to everybody and everybody loves to talk to him.

- Always smiling.

- He spreads positivity across the entire community. Great to see.

- It would be a great loss if Konrad didn't go to Marshall Community Center.

- The real magic is that he is always wanting others to be loved and cared for.

- The hardest part was watching him try to get a job.

- Konrad is always grateful and is a joy and an inspiration.

We had a nice visit with Brandon. Thank you very much Brandon for all your kind words!

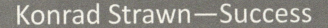

Konrad Strawn—Success

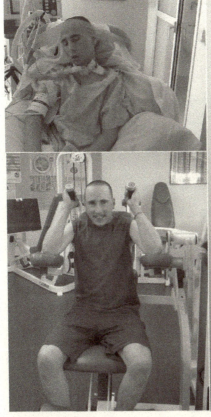

Hi, my name is Konrad.

I had an AVM, Arteriovenous Malformation. An AVM is an abnormal connection between the arteries and the veins in my brain. The rupture occurred on February 24, 2012, which led to a stroke. The stroke caused aphasia, a language disorder which effects the production or comprehension of speech and the ability to read or write. My entire right side had weakness and I was unable to see out of my right eye. I started learning all over again as if I were a baby. I was unable to talk for six weeks. The very first thing I said was "I love you."

My Physical Therapist, Chris, trained me on how to correctly use the equipment in a weight room. Once I was feeling better and having enough strength, I joined Marshall Community Center in May of 2013. I am here almost every day of the week, working out in the weight room, attending yoga classes and swimming. I find that I am improving my strength, endurance, balance and flexibility. I am continuing to recover and see changes, sometimes weekly. I have made many new friends, which makes it that much easier to come to Marshall.

My goal is to recover completely so that I can find the perfect job opportunity that fits my needs.

I will never give up. Miracles continue to happen all around me.

Thank you for all your support!

CITY OF
Vancouver
WASHINGTON
Parks & Recreation

VISIT www.vanparksrec.org
CALL 360-487-7090

One of the managers named Louise took notice of Konrad and wanted to use him as a success story to promote Marshall Community Center. This is a picture of what she created. It was a poster on the wall for a few years.

A Clark County Talk reporter noticed it and inspired her to write an article about Konrad for the online newspaper. Konrad keeps copies of it in a poster tube for his backpack and loves to take it everywhere and show it to anyone willing to read it.

12

An Unqualified Existence

The BIRC team also got Konrad started on the job hunting process. This was a lengthy process, over 400 applications and 40 interviews. Konrad was an expert at filling out applications and interviewing. He started with the Division of Vocational Rehabilitation. (DVR) We had a check in meeting every 6 months with Helen Christensen for several years until he finally got a job. She was in charge of his Supplemental Security Income. (SSI) She let us know how many hours he could work and still get Medicaid benefits. These were very interesting and important meetings. Konrad started at the Val Ogden Center to learn how to search for a job. He got job leads and filled out countless applications. He had over 40 job interviews before he finally got a job. He spent two days a week there searching for job leads. On the off days he was at Marshall Center working out, taking classes and hanging out talking to people. The more he talked to people the better he got at communicating. A job coach was assigned to him. Kelly Groen was his job coach for four years. She moved on to other things and then Konrad worked with Josh for a while. He probably would've gotten a job at Good Will but he had a felony that made getting a job a little more challenging. He also volunteered at The Quarry which is an assisted living facility. He loved that volunteer opportunity where he got to mingle with the residents and talk to people. His cousin Bill was working there at the time and that is why he got to volunteer there. Konrad was a bus boy there and loved visiting with the residents. They were going to hire him and had to do a background check, then sadly he had to stop working there because of his felony. They did write him a nice recommendation letter though.

Konrad has done a lot of volunteering. His first volunteer job was with the Backpack Program. His sister Roxann and I would drive him to a school where they would pack backpacks with food for the students to take home for the weekend and or evenings.

The next volunteer opportunity was with the Share Homestead, (emergency shelter). Two days a week for over four years Konrad helped prepare meals for the people that lived there temporarily to help them get back on their feet. Duties included food preparation and dishes. Some of the people that stayed there were very sad and some were determined to make the best of this opportunity to get help to find a job, by working with them on resumes and job applications. Konrad made many friends there. A few of them wrote beautiful letters of recommendations for him. It was a joy to take him to volunteer at the Share Homestead and to pick him up because he was always so happy about being able to help. One of his case managers wrote that his interactions with residents, other volunteers and staff were always polite, kind and very helpful. He is a born leader so helping direct other volunteers was a delight to him. He was always cheerful and friendly with staff.

Through SHARE he started volunteering for the Summer Meals Program. That would start around 8:00 in the morning till about 11:00 depending on how many volunteers showed up and how many lunches they had to prepare. He was always punctual and willing to perform any task. Since the stroke he is even more organized than he was before. Stocking is a great task for him. He did that as well as organizing materials, breaking down boxes, washing dishes, helping to expedite prepared meals, all while following health safety regulations, and keeping a positive attitude. Konrad and his dad still volunteer to help with the Summer Meal Program each summer on Konrad's days off. Before he got a job he would help every day. He loves helping the hungry kids.

The Habitat for Humanity was another place that Konrad volunteered. This was a midday job while Aidan was at school. He would help with donation drop off and customer service. He spent time reorganizing items to be sold, one of his great strengths. During his interview to volunteer there the manager Steve asked him about his initiative and he could not tell him about that. He had no idea what that meant. His job coach helped him with his resume where it talked about his initiative. He almost got a job there but the job at the VA came up. Konrad has a stack of wonderful letters of recommendation from the people he volunteered with over the years after the stroke while trying to get a real job.

Felony Vacated Finally! In 2018 after hours of filling out paperwork and many trips to the court house Konrad finally got his felony vacated. He had to have five years since he fulfilled all the court mandates from the trouble he got into. All fines paid, jail time served and community service completed. Vacating his record means that it will not be visible to anyone doing a background check on him. It does not completely get rid of it. If he were to get in trouble again then it would no longer be hidden from a background check. He tried to vacate his misdemeanor but the judge said that you can only vacate one criminal record. This was a game changer for the job seeking process. Kelly, his job coach, went with him to court to advocate for him. This was a very exciting day!

Someone along the way, probably one of his job coaches, discovered that he is half blind. He was eligible for Washington Vocational Services (WVS) with the Washington State Department of Services for the Blind. (DSB) WVS is yet another Community Rehabilitation Program (CRP) to help with Konrad's job search. There is a lot of help out there for disabled people. This was great. He got to work with another excellent counselor named Ardell Burns at DSB. She was my favorite person to go to monthly meetings to check in with. It was here that Konrad finally got a job. In 2017 he started to work with a job coach named Melissa. She was contracted through WVS. Helen Christensen signed the contract for Melissa to be Konrad's job coach. Helen oversees all of the job coaches Konrad worked with. Ardell recommended WVS. Ardell's clients use this vendor. This is where things really started to get hopeful.

His first real job was with The VA, The Veterans Administration. He was working in the kitchen serving the patients and making sure things were all right with their rooms and getting food orders. His title was Ambasador. Konrad loved this job. He had a fancy uniform that he wore proudly and looked quite sharp in. He had to use a computer but his disabilities were too great for this job. His job coach was supposed to help him until he could do the job. She was not allowed to do that because he was working with patients in a restricted area where she was not allowed to go. He was so proud of that job. Unfortunately he was too slow for the fast paced work that was required of him. It was devastating to lose this opportunity after trying so hard for so long to get a job. It was not long before he got another opportunity to go to work.

Ambassador

13

Hired

After he lost the job at the VA Konrad was so sad that he asked Helen if there was a closer vendor that he could work with, and have a different job coach that was closer to home where he could ride his bike to go and fill out applications and keep searching for a job. Ashley was Konrad's new job coach with First Choice Services until he wrongly used the "word of the day" and offended her. Identity was the word and she thought that he was telling her not to take his identity. He said, "You stole my identity." She was asking too many questions I guess. Whoops. They had met at Lifeline Connections for his job interview. He used C-VAN for his ride that day. She was so mad she just left. Jesse brought Konrad back to that campus later the same day to do a UA, and if he passed then he was hired. So then a woman named Teri Fears took over as his job coach. Konrad's new job was on the same campus as the VA. Lifeline Connections is where people go to detox off drugs and alcohol. There is an inpatient treatment as well as an outpatient program. Food is offered in the outreach program that serves homeless people while encouraging them to try to get sober. Konrad gets to make peanut butter and jelly sandwiches for the homeless people.

This was a miracle that led to writing this book, and Konrad getting to share where his experience, hope and his strength come from. This job is an example of God doing what God does. After hundreds of applications and dozens of interviews this is the place he ended up. All things happen for a reason. Teri helped him through the testing and stayed with him after the main training. She came to support him at his new job a couple times a week until he could perform all his duties successfully. He mostly does dishes but he is a very valuable part of the team. He is completely delighted when he gets to prepare food. Making peanut butter and frozen jam sandwiches makes him so happy. He is most frustrated when he has to do all the dishes or large pans by hand because of a too small dishwasher. He trained at the Women's Center where the dishwasher was too small to accommodate the large sheet pans. A Cook Aide like Konrad wanted to work at the Women's Center instead of the Men's Center, so Konrad got moved to the Men's Center and has been there for over five years. There is a nice big commercial dishwasher there. He is very grateful for that.

Recovered alcoholics and addicts are given an opportunity to work after the residential part of treatment. Chri A. is the manager and is quite compassionate with these employees that are part of a program called Business Venture. He gives them a few chances because relapses are so common. This program lasts for two years as long as they can stay sober. Then you can actually become a real employee. Konrad likes to come up with his own helpful ideas, but he mostly just follows orders and doesn't argue. He has had to learn to just do as he is told. For the first few years his yearly work performance reviews were not as positive as they have been since Konrad has been sharing his experience and hope so openly and passionately and doing what he is told. We would have to come up with goals for him and it was always about communication. Following directions is very important if you want to get along with your boss. He understands the health regulations and has come up with ideas to save money and keep people safe from contamination. For example, raw meat was stored right next to disposable plates and silverware. He has taken over our refrigerator as well and makes sure things are stored correctly. This was a little frustrating at first but we just gave up and went with his organizing efforts.

The assistant manager/cook, Mike Olson, has worked closely with Konrad from the beginning. He was kind enough to give us a call and talk about how nice it is to work with Konrad. This is what Mike had to say about working with Konrad.

- Konrad is a wonderful human being.

- He always remembers names.

- Konrad is super friendly.

- He cares about everything.

- Great young man, great soul.

- Very good success story.

- He didn't know the names of utensils in the beginning.

- Konrad is an inspiration to clients.

- He has come a long way.

Thank you Mike for calling to tell us what a great guy Konrad is.

About a year after Konrad's employment at Lifeline Connections, an employee at the time, possibly a social worker or counselor, read Konrad's Success Story from Marshall Community Center. She loved it so much that she laminated it and hung it on the bulletin board. She also read the

Article that was written by Clark County Talk, an online news source. Susan was a reporter from Clark County Talk and saw the Success Story that was posted at Marshall Community Center and wanted to write an article about Konrad. This opened the door for Konrad to share that article with anyone and everyone that would read it. Konrad even bought poster tubes so he could bring his article with him to share with people. He approached a lady named Tammy at Marshall Community Center to read his article and she was very excited and told him that he should write a book. That was the seed that was planted and has become a reality.

So Konrad's article eventually led to him speaking on a panel once a month to the guys in the residential section of Lifeline Connections where he works. Now that is one of his favorite things to do. Who would've thought that a young man that almost died could come back and make a difference to the people that are trying to better their lives. Not just at these panel meetings, but any time he comes across the clients he encourages them.

14

Heart Wrenching Desperation

Someone that was very close to him is quite disgusted that he is being put up on a pedestal now, when he "Was always the villain." The writing of this book has brought up a lot of painful memories for people that are close to Konrad. A person close to us called and was in crisis recently, which painted a very clear picture of what it is like to see a loved one struggling with addiction to drugs and alcohol. Thank God my husband and I are a safe place to come to instead of going home and blowing your brains out. The desperation from how much it hurts us, compounded by knowing that the person in the middle of the addiction is suffering even more, is too much to bear alone. Often the suffering addict is full of self hate and disgust at themselves and the pain they cause others. The pain and fear of losing our loved one is beyond our control. Seeing someone in crisis like this is gut wrenching. So many big emotions! We were at a loss to tell them what to do. The fact is, I can barely control myself let alone try to force someone else to stop their destructive dangerous behavior. Essentially we can not make *anyone* do anything that they don't want to or are not ready to do. Praying a lot and loving them doesn't feel like we are doing all that we possibly can. Trying to not enable our loved ones is one of the hardest things to do.

During one of the meetings the family was invited to while Konrad was in treatment, we were told to love our son in a detached way. Much easier said than done, even though that is probably easier to do with a child than with a significant other. This is so hard. The struggle is real! All I could say is "Don't give up!" The fear and worry that your loved one may not make it home alive is heart wrenching, time consuming and exhausting.

One of Konrad's counselors told him to imagine the person you love more than anyone else in the whole world finding you dead from an overdose or suicide. When I first heard this, it seemed like it would be profoundly helpful.

15

Konrad's Transportation

In 2017 Uncle Scott gave Konrad a bicycle to ride. Uncle Scott had a work injury and hurt his hip. He has never been the same. He won this bike at a picnic and after hurting his hip could not ride it anymore. So he fixed it up and gave it to Konrad to ride. Konrad's main transportation to the gym and work was C-VAN for 5 years. Now he doesn't ever ride the bus. He uses his bike to go work and to Marshall Center to work out. He loves Gentle Yoga, Flow Yoga and the pool classes. He hasn't done the pool classes or the Yoga classes since the pandemic. He tried Zumba Gold for elderly folks but it was too loud and fast paced for his liking. He likes a class that used to be called Total Body Blast but now it is called Mindful Movement.

I get the pleasure of driving him to work on the snowy days because my Subaru is so good in the snow and ice. I really enjoy driving around in the snow unless there are fools driving recklessly. I was paid to be a caregiver until around 2019. I took him shopping every week which was about a three hour venture. He was my boss so he had no problem having me take him to several different stores to find the best prices. Except for that one particular grocery store, because he couldn't go in there for 100 years. One day shortly after he came home from the hospital we went past Albertsons grocery store because I thought that he would not remember that he wasn't supposed to go into the other store, but we pulled in there and he wagged his finger at me and communicated "No!" I was surprised and disappointed. After my hysterectomy in 2018 he did go into that store with me that he was banned from so he could push the cart for me because I wasn't supposed to lift more than 5 pounds. I was shocked and pleasantly surprised. Usually he just waits in the car if I want to go in there. That's a good post surgery memory.

There have been many trips to the bike repair shop and a few replacement bikes since that bike Uncle Scott gave him. He even had one that was stolen. On his way to work one morning he thought he could get through a four lane street on a yellow light and a lady crashed right into him. He had a big gash in his leg but not too bad overall. That was the end of Uncle Scott's bike. The hospital kept him overnight just in case, because they decided not to do a CT scan due to the fact that he has had enough of those in his lifetime already. He had to get a new bike after that.

He crashed going up a trail one day when he encountered another biker speeding down the hill and they collided. Neither one of them were hurt thankfully. Another day he was going down a hill and enjoying the sights and pressed the brake too hard and put his teeth through his lip. That was his first mishap while riding his bike. He has been making his angels work overtime. One morning he was riding very fast going down a steep hill in morning traffic on his way to work and a van was crowding the bike lane and he narrowly avoided a deadly crash. He was probably going 30 or 40 miles per hour.

In April of 2023 he was almost home just peddling away and there was a pickup truck coming out of their apartment complex and Konrad noticed that he was looking at his phone. He did not stop coming out of his driveway and BOOM, he ran right into him. It was the most painful crash up until February of 2025. He should have gotten some kind of compensation for the pain and suffering but the driver didn't have any insurance or something. The sheriff at the scene gave us a case number on his business card but we were never able to acquire a copy of the accident report. My insurance company could not get a copy of the accident report either with the information the sheriff gave me. He got a ride in the ambulance that day. The wind really got knocked out of him. He was having trouble breathing. He had several ribs that were fractured and he was very sore for a few months. My auto insurance replaced his bike once again and his medical insurance paid for the hospital visit and ambulance ride. He is on his fourth bike in six years. This bike he has had since May 2023. His helmet lights and bicycle lights are very bright and flash in a rather annoying way. He is very visible these days! The front headlight has an option that is so bright that cars will flash their bright lights at him. Konrad would use his bike to do his grocery shopping if he could.

After the social worker visit in 2019 he was deemed too independent to qualify for care giving services. I lost my caregiving job. About that same time my parents moved into an assisted living home and I spent a lot of time taking care of my mom. She was on kidney dialysis which meant a lot of trips to get procedures to keep that going. Konrad's dad retired about that time too so he started to take Konrad shopping weekly and to various appointments.

His dad stepped in just in time to work on getting a leg brace that was comfortable enough to use while at work. He has been trying to get his leg brace comfortable and went to get it adjusted or replaced about 24 times in two years. We are still working on getting something more comfortable. The oldest brace is the one that is the most comfortable but not perfect. The brace helps him move around a little faster with less chance of tripping from the foot drop on the right side. It helps with his gait somewhat and lessens the chance of falling.

2/10/25 Konrad loves to ride his bike to Marshall Community Center to work out. On this particular morning there was an odd frost on the ground. I walked outside and tested how slippery it was. It was strangely not slick. Well, Konrad did the same thing and decided it would be safe to ride his bike to go and work out. As he was rounding the corner, coasting toward Marshall Community Center at about 20 miles per hour and hit some black ice and took a very hard spill. On the corner of Fort Vancouver Way and McLoughlin Boulevard there is usually a puddle from the rain. But not this morning, it was solid ice! It was hard enough to break the femur bone at the hip joint. He broke the biggest bone in the human body. It took until the end of April, about six weeks, before he could start to work on going up and down the stairs. Konrad started with one trip up and down the stairs to the basement each day. It has been a VERY painful healing process. It's six months now and Konrad is still not able to go back to work. Dr. Amitai said it would be eight months to a year, I guess he really meant that, even with someone as active and determined as Konrad.

At the scene of the accident he was instantly surrounded by people he knew. One of his friends from Marshall Community Center named Bob along with 2 other people carried him off the street onto the curb. He could not bend his leg. One of them happened to be a paramedic. There was a woman too. Bob was kind enough to take Konrad's bike for him. He later took it to Portland and had it checked over and cleaned up to make sure it was in good working order. He also bought a new helmet for him just in case he had hit his head.

The paramedic asked if he could check his hip and he didn't think it was broken. The woman was concerned about the expense of an ambulance and tried to talk him out of calling 911. Konrad insisted that he needed medical help. The pain was close to a 10 on a scale of 1-10. The woman called for an ambulance and it arrived in less than five minutes. Because of the ice there wasn't much abrasion but lots of pain in the knee and hip. Konrad called his dad but he was in Longview for a reunion breakfast with the retired guys he had worked with. I got a call at work but also didn't answer my phone because I was working. I left work and went to the hospital where we stayed till late in the evening until after the surgery was over. Dr. Ari D. Amitai, one of the best orthopedic surgeons, did the surgery. He said it was not your everyday 80 year old hip fracture. He would have to make it perfect for a thirty six year old very active young man. While we were talking to the anesthesiologist, one of them mentioned that his leg would be a little shorter because of the way that the bone shrinks up as it heals. I thought, "OH NO! His leg is already shorter from the spasticity due to the stroke." The surgery took much longer than the usual 20 minute fixation for a typical hip fracture patient. Dr. Amitai said it may take longer than usual and he would call us if it did. The usual fixation part of the surgery is typically about 20 minutes. After about two hours into the surgery he called us to let us know that it was taking much longer because he wanted to get it perfect for a young active person that wanted to live a long time pain free. The surgeon was going to fix it with a plate and rod with screws, however, the flat part of the inside of the femur was also fractured so he could not use a plate, since the flat part of the inside of the upper femur is where he was going to attach the plate. So Konrad now has a rod down his right leg with two screws. Dr. Amitai told us when he came to talk to us after the surgery that Konrad was going to be very sore, and not from the fracture either. He had 25 stitches on the outside and some on the inside as well.

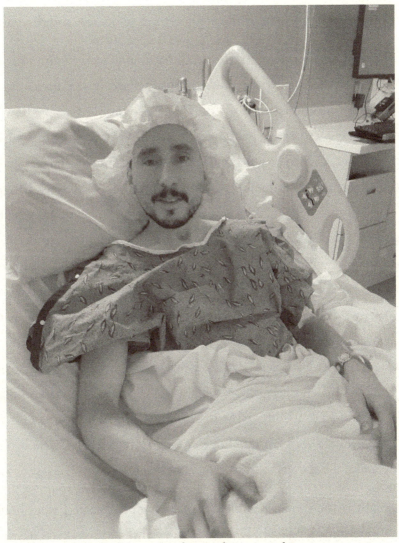

Konrad in his party hat on his way to hip surgery

Konrad spent six days in the hospital, partly waiting for a bed to open in a skilled nursing facility, and partly because we had a little snow storm that delayed things for a day or two. He was a great patient full of gratitude instead of grouchiness. He was a favorite patient of the staff. The people in charge wanted to send him home because he could walk with the walker just fine and stand on one foot to brush and floss his teeth. We were concerned because of the language deficit that he would not be able to follow the directions given by the medical team of doctors and therapists.

Meals at the hospital were pretty good. I was able to bring him his big bowl of veggies and an avocado and the hospital provided a nice chunk of grilled salmon to add to it for the protein. I also brought his big bowl of blueberries. His dad and I spent our days with him at the hospital during that week's stay.. When he went to Brookfield skilled nursing facility I went back to work until he came home. It had been a very long week hanging out at the hospital all day. We were advocating for a skilled nursing facility because of his aphasia. We wanted to make sure he completely understood what he could and could not do. He ended up at Brookfield Health and Rehabilitation of Cascadia. Kaiser said he could stay for 7 to 10 days but the social worker said he had unlimited skilled nursing because of being on medicaid. After three weeks Kaiser said he was being discharged and we could appeal if we wanted to. By then Konrad had gotten a roommate that was grouchy and left the lights on at night. He kept the TV so loud at night that Konrad had to use his earplugs. He was yelling to his son in his sleep and complained about Konrad hogging the sink etc. He had also broken his hip and did not even want to get out of bed to eat.

Each night I would help Konrad get ready for bed before I went home. Those were some long days! I worked all day and spent my evenings with Konrad. The first evening that I went to see him at Brookfield I got to speak to the Physical Therapist and told him that Konrad wanted to do 3 hours of physical therapy every day. He grinned real big and said that his supervisor did not mind if he spent extra time with the patients. I brought him his blueberries each evening and an avocado but not his big bowl of veggies. Konrad eats very clean so the normal diet that people were eating at Brookfield was disappointing for him.

One Sunday afternoon I got to help out a lot. I got to be a caregiver and get him ready for bed, a hair stylist and gave him a haircut and shave, and a plumber as I fixed the toilet in the bathroom in his room. The chain had come loose and there was poop from someone else left in the toilet, and then I used the toilet, at this point I was determined to get it to flush. I knew what was wrong right away but didn't really want to put my hand into the tank on the back of the toilet and hook the chain back up. After a few hours I just rolled up my sleeve and took care of it.

Konrad's dad and I put together several jigsaw puzzles while he was at Brookfield. His dad worked on them during the day and I worked on them in the evening until it was time to get Konrad ready for bed. He missed the food at home. He was finally ready to go home when he got a roommate. His stay was a little less enjoyable after that. He lost about 9 pounds in that month because he wouldn't eat some of the foods there, like the bread.

When he came home he had to sit on a shower bench to take a shower. We borrowed one from my mother in law. It was really cool. The bench slides on this rail to get him from the outside of the tub to the inside. We could not figure out how it worked because the seat would not stay in the upright position. It kept falling backwards. We prayed about it and the answer came to us at the same time. It was missing 2 bolts because it had been moved a few times. We had trouble figuring out how it worked because the 2 bolts that were missing secured the seat and kept it from falling backwards. Jesse went to the hardware store and got replacement bolts to fix it and then it worked great. It took about two and a half months until he was mostly standing. He used the shower bench to get in and out of the tub for 5 months. Finally, with a lot of determination and caution he was done with it. Now he can take a shower like a normal person.

Two weeks after the surgery he got the stitches taken out and strips of tape were put on to hold the seam together. The strips would just fall off. After his shower one night I asked if the strips were going down the drain because they would plug up the drain. Konrad's eyes got real big and he said, "I don't know, they just left." That cracked me up. I found one on the kitchen floor and one in the laundry so I was hoping they weren't going down the drain.

It took five and a half months before he tried riding his bike again. Hopefully he won't ride it when it's icy out anymore. My husband is so frustrated that Konrad's dad and I let him ride his bike at all. "After all he is half blind and can't drive a car so why are we letting him ride a bike! Don't you guys care? If that was my kid he wouldn't be riding a bike on the busy streets at all!" Great logic but you can't take away someone's independence when they are stubborn and insistent! He rode his bike to Marshall Community Center again six months after the accident. He was absolutely delighted to see everyone there after being stuck at home for so long.

16

Post Stroke Routines

BOOKS! Konrad loves to read books, especially history books. My Uncle Dean recommended a bunch of books for him. Some of them are huge. The book about Ulysses S. Grant is 959 pages. He has one about Truman that is 992 pages long. A friend at Marshall Center gave him a book about the political genius of Abraham Lincoln, and it is 748 pages long. One of his pilate classmates brought him a book called The Blind Woodsman. It's a book about a man who is blind because he tried to kill himself with a gun. Konrad loved that book.

When he started learning to read again he highlighted all the words he didn't know with a yellow highlighter. Most of the pages were highlighted in the beginning. His first chapter book after the stroke was given to him by his speech therapist, Julie. It is very highlighted, looking at it now there are still lots of words that should have been highlighted. "A Mouse Called Wolf" by Dick King-Smith. A sentence described an orange cat's tail using the word ginger, as far as he knows that is a spice he recently experimented with in his cereal for breakfast. Along with turmeric. Sounds pretty yucky to me. He said he wasn't going to buy those spices again. Now he uses his phone and looks up the words to get the definition and pronunciation. He reads books when he is not doing something else. Definitely his number one hobby.

Routine is still a big part of his life. He doesn't like to change his routine much. Unfortunately for us he was going to bed around 7:30 pm and got up at 3:33 am in the morning for YEARS! Konrad getting up in the middle of the night has been very disruptive to our sleep. Since his last bike accident he doesn't have to go to work so we finally convinced him to move his sleeping schedule up an hour. This has been a real struggle for him. This has been a great relief for the light sleeper in our home. As our protector, Jesse is tuned into any strange noises at night and wakes up easily. We should have put our foot down in the beginning. I felt sad that Konrad was missing out on the evening time with his son but thought that this weird schedule was just more post-stroke aftereffects. As we get older we can't do without sleep because of being woken up with thumping over our heads from exercising or pots and pans rattling around, the garage door opening and closing etc. Konrad was deeply disappointed that he had to cut out his exercising in the mornings before work by getting up later, but we are very thankful. We will get through this adjustment in his schedule. Getting him to stay in bed later before the hip fracture was a big fight, as he didn't want to give up that time to exercise before work. I hope he doesn't try to go back to getting up at 3:30 am when he gets back to work.

He spends about one and a half hours preparing a king's breakfast of grains that take up to an hour to cook. He has a large bowl of yogurt with blueberries, figs, cashews, ground flax seeds, banana, pumpkin seeds, pistachios, and cacao powder as an appetizer. In the 1 ½ quart saucepan of 14 different kinds of grains he adds cacao powder, sweet potato, peanut butter, cashews, almonds, pistachios, walnuts, pumpkin seeds, banana, figs, cinnamon, matcha powder and milk. Then, in his green tea he adds chia seeds and hemp hearts. He does not drink anything except multiple kinds of tea throughout the day and relaxing sleepy-time teas before bed.

Since his latest stay at the skilled nursing facility he has started drinking coffee because he was so tired from trying to go to sleep there. It was quite noisy there with beepers and loud TV's etc. He doesn't want to see me pour extra coffee down the sink. Jesse and I like our coffee dark and strong. He drank about a half a pot of leftover coffee one Sunday morning and was so jittery his heart and mind were racing. He didn't know what was going on. He keeps my leftover coffee in the fridge now and doesn't drink quite so much. Now I make sure there is some left for him to drink.

For lunch he eats like a prince, a big bowl of fresh veggies that he prepares ahead of time on Sunday mornings for the week. He adds a protein of fish, or chicken. He adds beans to his salad that he cooks in the biggest pots I have and then freezes them in containers like he does with his fish and chicken. This food prep usually happens on Sunday mornings for the week and beyond, depending on the food item. His son gets mostly frozen pre-prepared foods because that's what he wants. Konrad just doesn't "offer" fresh fruits and veggies unless Aidan puts them on the grocery list, because he can't stand it when they don't get eaten and have to be thrown away. At seventeen, Aidan is getting better about putting the food he wants to eat on the list. Aidan has been eating the meals we prepare a lot more nowadays too. That makes me happy. Eating together as a family is a tradition I value deeply. Feeding Aidan healthy food has been one of the hardest parts of being guardians. The parental dynamics are difficult at times. Konrad can do most of the parenting but it is difficult to know for sure when he needs support. We have fruit around that he can eat but we don't eat very much fresh fruits and veggies either. We juice our veggies mostly, which Aidan drinks occasionally. He was putting a boiled egg on his salad for lunch but since we got chickens he doesn't like to eat those anymore. They don't peel well at all when they are so fresh and they make his stomach feel weird. Konrad also eats an apple and an avocado with his lunch.

For dinner if you want to call it that he eats like a rich pauper. He eats about 1 ½ pounds of semi-frozen blueberries at 3:30 pm. He exercises and then does quite a regime of regular flossing, uses a Waterpik and then he brushes his teeth. After he cleans his teeth he gets on the computer to read his emails and shops. He would be a great professional shopper. He just purchased a new freezer for us that we split the cost for. I told him that I wasn't going to have anything to do with getting a new freezer, that was going to be up to you guys. So he got online and bought one from Costco and told us that it was going to be delivered on Saturday, and they were going to take the old one away. He sat at the kitchen table, where you'll often find him, while I helped the delivery guys figure out how to get the freezer down the stairs. Jesse had to come home from his friend's house and take off the door handle because none of the delivery guys or us knew how to get the door off with the fancy self-closing hinges.

So, after shopping and emails Konrad reads books or practices his language skills in his aphasia workbook, then he takes a shower at 7:00 pm. It's pretty much bedtime after that. This is what post stroke life is like thirteen years later.

Since Aidan was about eight years old he was expected to put the food on a list that he wanted for that week. He couldn't of course, so if he was willing to eat what we were eating that was great. But most of the time he didn't want to eat what we were eating. Especially for the year and a half when we were eating vegan because of my cancer diagnosis. That was my follow up treatment after my hysterectomy rather than radiation. Beans, beans, and more beans. Aidan just wasn't into that! Konrad tries feeding him breakfast in the mornings before school but he doesn't want to eat that either. His best school year was in second grade when he ate one or two waffles made from Kodiak Cakes Flapjack and Waffle mix. There is a freezer full of microwave food for Aidan to eat. At seventeen he is getting pretty good at feeding himself. He eats a lot after we have all gone to bed. He is "nocturnal" after all. Aidan is a great host and brings his friends over to eat pizza and whatever else is in the freezer. He brings a bag of food when he goes to his friend's house. Jesse just taught him how to use the BBQ. He cooked a delicious venison burger for himself and Jesse recently.

It is very tricky for Aidan with a disabled parent that insists on taking care of his son. Early on the people at BIRC told us that Konrad could stay home alone with his son as long as there was a list of phone numbers accessible. It never felt quite right leaving Konrad home alone with a six year old. I can't say that we feel particularly good about the care we all gave Aidan as he was growing up. His Aunt Roxann said the same thing not long ago. It feels like we could've done better. I work until around 7:00 pm most evenings, so that left the guys to try to do schoolwork and dinner by themselves. It has been challenging to say the least. I can't even imagine doing this without Jesus and the guiding comfort of the Holy Spirit.

17

Be Encouraged, There is Hope

I had been looking for just the right words to bring this inspiring story to a close, when Konrad brought me his journal from right before his stroke when he was reading the Bible every day and journaling. It is a miracle that his dad did not throw it out along with most of his other books and stuff when cleaning out the house after it finally sold. So, here it is in his own words, a few months before his one year clean and sober date and life changing stroke.

Last journal entry before getting clean and sober.

1/17/2011 – Emergency room visit for infection on right shoulder. What a way to spend my birthday.

9/29/2011 <u>Genesis 1:1-2:3</u> – So begins A 365 Day Plan to Read this big ass book!

9/30/2011 <u>Genesis 2:15-3:24</u> – Even reading this little bit I can feel it in my stomach and chest. It's an overwhelming sensation. I very much look forward to understanding Christianity and God's Word.

10/1/11 <u>Genesis 4:1-16</u> – I'm going to try to worship God out of LOVE and not out of duty or need.

10/2/2011 <u>Genesis 6:9-22</u> – I think Noah may have been on a ship with animal DNA. I do believe in an ancient Mesa Flood.

10/3/2011 <u>Genesis 7:1-24</u> – I open myself, heart, mind, body, Spirit, soul and everything else God has a use for. I surrender my will to God so He can build me into something great. I will do the best I can with what I have and let God handle the things I can not. Reading the Bible makes me feel good in my chest this morning and it's exactly what I needed.

Thank you Lord

10/4/2011 <u>Genesis 8:1-22</u> – Ten and a half months is a long time on a boat, even if it's a huge yacht without animals of every kind. The Earth would be a really quiet place with all living things having been completely wiped out.

I pray that I will not have to live through an apocalypse myself.

10/5/2011 <u>Genesis 9:1-17</u> – I wonder if God gave man rainbows by letting him see more colors <u>in</u> his eyes. So far I have really enjoyed reading this book. I feel the power of God's Words and I am growing closer to Him every day.

10/6/2011 <u>Genesis 11:1-9</u> – The Tower of Babel was just part of a city where everyone spoke the same language until God said "Look" and changed their languages so the people scattered across the world. Why? I wonder what was really going on then?

10/7/2011 <u>Genesis 12:1-9; 17:1-8; 15-16</u> – Wow! God sure had Abraham do a lot and in return protected him and blessed him. I'm willing to do what God asks of me to the best of my ability. As I learn more about God

I feel more inclined to trust in Him. It's a nice feeling to have Jesus and God's Word as well as a growing faith in Christianity.

10/8/2011 <u>Genesis 18:1-15</u> – If I met three strangers I probably would be polite but if they told me my 90 something year old wife would have a baby I myself would most likely laugh. I do believe that nothing is too hard for the Lord. It's just hard for me to truly believe in something I do not feel, see, touch, hear, smell, or understand fully yet. I *do* want to believe though so I am going to keep investigating God's Word and try my best to put it into action in my life.

Thank you for being a God I can question about Jesus and Father. Amen

10/9/2011 <u>Genesis 19:1-29</u> – Wow! In all of Sodom and Gomorrah there were not even ten righteous people. The men who tried to force themselves on Lot and his visiting angels and family are just insanely horny or sexually corrupt like I've never known. I believe it was necessary for God to cleanse the two sick ass cities. I hope Jesus can truly forgive my sins.

I ask for strength to remain turned or changed (repented) from the man I have been. Thank you for the mercy I've received Lord. Let me be an instrument to your will from now on. Amen

10/10/2011 <u>Genesis 21:8-21</u> – Abraham is very obedient and trusting towards God. He let Hagar and Ishmael go off into the desert wilderness with very little supplies like Sarah and God asked. God protected them personally just like he said he would. I'm grateful God has watched over me in my darkest moments. I feel like God has a personal interest in my life as well. I may be wrong, but I think God does love me specifically.

So, thank you Lord.

10/11/2011 <u>Genesis 22:1-19</u> – Being willing to do ANYTHING for God is who Abraham clearly was. I'm willing to be honest, open minded, and willing but I would have a very hard time attempting to sacrifice my only son. This shows that God will test my faith more than likely at some point in a big way. I do believe that God, Jesus and the Holy Spirit know what's best for me.

I'm asking to have knowledge of God's will for me and the power to carry it out. Amen

10/12/2011 <u>Genesis 24:1-27</u> – This was a well written entertaining passage to read. Abraham's servant is a good man and Isaac is one lucky man to have a virgin wife who is beautiful inside and out as a surprise one day. I am very blessed to have the kind of life I have today. I do believe that God has watched over me and now I am an instrument of his will. My plan is to keep reading the Bible, praying, go to Alpha class and begin doing other good works like donating time/$ to charity.

10/13/2011 <u>Genesis 25:19-34</u> – Esau and Jacob do not seem to value each other for love or brotherhood. Esau had to be absolutely starved to trade his birthright for stew. Jacob is just conniving and desperate for power. What he did strikes me as wrong and I wonder what he was feeling and thinking that would drive him to do such a thing. My sister and I used to fight a lot but we never took anything permanently from each other. Thank God we have grown out of our fighting ways and after I honestly apologized and she accepted as well as returned a sincere apology we are friends today and brother/sister. My faith in God and Christianity is going up and down like waves right now but I'm going to remain honest, open minded and willing to continue to read the Bible, do my daily meditation, pray, attend Alpha class, ask others, NA/AA, outpatient and maybe church. I'm asking God to let me know He is for real and that Jesus is for real. I want meaning in my life, and to go to Heaven with Jesus is a good motivation.

Please God, show me the truth. Amen

10/14/2011 Genesis 27:1-40 – That is some sneaky shit Jacob and Rebekah pulled on Isaac and Esau. I know at times a blessing like this may seem worth stealing but deep down a part of me would say this sort of thing is just wrong. I am asking God to show me the best plan of action for my life and to help me do his will and not my self-centered will. Things always work out better when I listen to my conscience as well as I feel better about my self esteem and integrity.

Thank you for your help in my life's works Lord Jesus. Amen

10/15/2011 Genesis 28:10-22 – I have had to find my own religion, God, faith, spirituality, just as Jacob did. My mustard seed of faith is growing in Christ.

I pray that God will fill me with the Holy Spirit and help me to continue to grow in my faith. I want something righteous to believe in badly. Amen

10/16/2011 Genesis 29:14-30 – Jacob loved Rachel enough to work for 7+7 years to marry her. He was tricked into marrying Rachel's older sister after all that time by his father in law by using a veil over Leah's face and he had children with her, but continued to love Rachel most. He also had two concubines named Bilhah and Zilpah. Now that sounds like true love to me. I try to show my love by honesty, obedience, service, kindness, protection, and companionship as I learn to love God and understand his love for me. I grow excited to have a real relationship with God.

Jesus please come into my self-body, mind, soul, being etc. and be my captain. Amen

10/17/2011 <u>Genesis 32:1-38, 33:18</u> – This is a good example of how time and sincere apology can help bring a brother and brother who were bitterly divided back together. Jacob left for 20 years and when he finally returned home everything turned out ok. He tried to make things right and prayed for God's help and it all worked out.

God help me to face my problems head on with your help and not procrastinate. Amen

10/18/2011 <u>Genesis 37</u> – Jacob's son Joseph, being sold into slavery, is a story I remember vaguely. It's well written. I take it as a reminder of what jealousy left unchecked can lead us to do. Also, I love what happens later when Joseph takes all the hardships and uses them to his best advantage. Still, I just can't imagine what it must have felt like to be sold into slavery by your own brothers.

Thank you God for watching over me in times of good decisions and helping me deal with bad situations. Amen

10/19/2011 *It's been three weeks <u>Genesis 39</u> – God was truly with Joseph in everything he did. Even as a slave the Lord blessed him with faithful love. Joseph maintained a good attitude even after Potifar's wife tried to sleep with him and told her husband that Joseph was going to rape her when he refused her advances. He was then thrown into prison, and even in prison the Lord was with him and he made the best of it all.

I humbly ask the Lord Jesus and God to fill me with the Holy Spirit and help me to continue to make the best of what I've got and to always be grateful for what I have received. Thank you Lord for your guidance and giving me hope for me and my family's future. Amen

10/20/2011 <u>Genesis 40</u> – Joseph helped the chief cupbearer out by interpreting his dream in prison and when he got out he was supposed to help Joseph to be released. Instead he forgot all about Joseph. In my addiction there were times where people would do me favors and ask for help in return and I would just ditch them and vice versa. These last 8 months I've accomplished a lot and I'm coming to believe, trust, understand and give the glory and much gratitude to my higher power that runs my new life and will completely. I've chosen to call my higher power Jesus, God and Holy Spirit. I'm a christian now and I'm really enjoying it.

10/21/2011 <u>Genesis 41:1-36</u> – After 2 more years Joseph finally gets out of prison for a bit to go see Pharaoh and interpret his dreams. Joseph strikes me as a blessed individual and one who believes 100% in God. He walks with God and gives God much glory whenever possible. Even during a prison term he has faith and <u>patience.</u>

God please help me grow my mustard seed of faith and to produce good fruit for you, so that I can become like Joseph and trust/love you always with patience and 100% doubtless belief in you. Amen

10/22/2011 <u>Genesis 41:37-57</u> – Thanks to God, Joseph did very well and his knowledge of the oncoming famine was vital to many people's lives. His life was good thanks to God and his obedience. He kept doing the next right thing.

Thank you Lord for helping me come out of my very serious mistakes. Please help me to find/make success out of my life. Let me do your will. Amen

10/23/2011 <u>Genesis 42</u> – Seeing the people who betrayed him and being in a place of great authority over them Joseph spoke harshly to them and put Simeon in prison until Joseph's youngest brother Benjamin and all the family came to see him. I'm guessing Joseph will be nice to his family when they return. It would be awfully tempting to be vengeful towards people who have betrayed me. I thank God for helping me to forgive and let go of my resentments.

Lord, please give me the wisdom on how to deal with old "friends" and the strength to not give in to any of their temptations. Amen

10/24/2011 <u>Genesis 43</u> – Fear is very strongly felt by Joseph's brothers and father as they return to Egypt for food with Benjamin. My guess is that Joseph will reveal himself and forgive them all pretty soon. If it was me I probably would've been harsh, and scared the brothers that sold me at first, but when they returned and apologized I'd let them know I forgive them.

Lord, help me to forgive the people who have hurt me in the past, present and future. Amen

10/25/2011 <u>Genesis 44</u> – This story has me very interested in what will happen next. I can relate to Judah. There was a time in my life when I was putting my own son and everyone else around me through dangerous hell-like situations. In the last 8 months I've become a new man who places great value on the people I love and I've totally transformed. No longer am I a strung out loser. All my troubles have brought me to the Lord who has given me something to worship.

I depend on you, Lord. You give great and satisfying peace. Thank you Lord Jesus. Amen

10/26/2011 <u>Genesis 45, 46:26-30</u> – Aidan is my only and most beloved son. If I were to lose him thinking he was dead for several years I would be devastated. The joy I imagine Jacob and his family felt when they found Joseph alive and very well, must have been overwhelming! I love how humble Joseph is when he says that everything happened according to God's will/plan and not his own. He gives God all the glory.

Lord let me be an instrument of your will and give you the glory where glory is due. Amen

10/27/2011 <u>Genesis 49</u> – I finished Genesis. One of my favorite books in the Bible. I look forward to finishing Exodus as well.

10/28/2011 <u>Exodus 1:8-2:10</u> – So begins another well written book in my Bible that I am thoroughly enjoying.

Thank you for helping me to be delivered from Heroin addiction and other awful things I was a slave to and worshipped in a way only Lord Jesus, God and the Holy Spirit should be worshipped. Please help me to be of some use to you today and another human being. I love you dearly Lord. Thank you. Amen

10/29/2011 <u>Exodus 2:11-25</u> – So Moses was no holy man. He was a murderer. God still used him for amazing things. My hope is that God can find a good use for myself and my certain talents.

10/30/2011 <u>Exodus 3</u> – "Jehovah or Yahweh is...My eternal name, my name to remember for all generations." Moses saw the very clear sign of God and became an excellent choice as he did everything God asked. I think.

Thank you Lord for showing yourself and your son to me slowly but surely. Please allow me (all that I am) to be of use to your needs and infinite wisdom. Amen

10/31/2011 <u>Exodus 4</u> – So Moses really was not sure what to do about the Lord's plan to save the Jews from slavery. God was almost ready to kill Moses until his wife circumcised their son? There are a couple of spots in the Bible that make me wonder what else is there in the missing books, you know things that have been hidden on purpose to avoid the truth in a way. I know how Moses feels in this chapter, sometimes I'm not sure what I can do for God. Often I feel like I'm doing the next right thing to the best of my ability and maybe that's all God wants of me? *Anyway, I love you God, Jesus, and Holy Spirit. Thank you for watching over me and listening to me and just being here for me Lord. Amen*

11/1/2011 <u>Exodus 5</u> – Pharaoh is a pretty crude man for punishing his slaves like this. It makes God's treatment of him seem appropriate. When Moses could not solve his problem he came to God again and told him what happened. I'm going to try Moses's technique and ask God, tell God, and listen to God.

Thank you for being there for me, Lord. Amen

11/2/2011 <u>Exodus 6:1-13</u> – Moses doubts himself and wants to hesitate in this whole mission. I can't say that I blame him in a way but still if Yahweh (God) asked me to do something I would try my best and focus on the solution.

Lord, thank you for your help and please let me know you, be righteous and of use to your plan. Amen

11/3/11 <u>Exodus 7:1-14</u> – I love how God explains why he hardens Pharaoh's heart. He does it in order to show the Egyptians the miracles of God. After reading this, what I read in Roman's makes more sense and doesn't make me feel as frustrated and confused.

Thank you Lord for revealing yourself to me today. It feels good to understand. Please allow me to understand you as best as I can. Amen

11/4/2011 <u>Exodus 7:15-9:7</u> – I imagine at this point Moses has 100% faith in God and God's power. After 5 plagues happening when and how God said they would, and starting and stopping just like God said, that would seem miraculous. Moses is the clearest example of God's very real, near and awesome power. I personally would be utterly amazed!

Thank you Lord for doing so many great miracles both big and small throughout my life and protecting me. Please let me be useful and good from now on to you and your will. Thanks so much! Amen

11/5/2011 <u>Exodus 9:8-10:29</u> – God hardened Pharaoh's heart in order to have things go according to plan. I wonder if Pharaoh will end up in Heaven? I have faced many consequences for my wrongdoing and these painful results have brought me to my knees firmly. Now that I have a relationship with God, Jesus and the Holy Spirit I feel as though I will be ok.

Thank you for being an understanding God who wants anything to do with me. Lord please help me to keep doing the next right thing. Amen

11/6/2011 <u>Exodus 11, 12:29-36</u> – I wonder how blood on the doors kept the Angel of Death out of the Israelites homes. 600.000 Jews is a lot of people to communicate these messages to so quickly. I can only imagine how these things happened. This last plague sure was a doozie, the sound of all the people crying over the death of their first born son would be deafening! God worked a lot of very impressive clear proofs of his existence. I wish I knew God like these people.

Thank you for loving, forgiving and letting me get to know you Lord. Please allow my faith to grow and my fruit be good. Amen

11/7/2011 Exodus 13:17-14:31 – This is one part of the Bible where as I read it and think about it I feel there was something extra-terrestrial involved with the pillars of fire and cloud. I do like the part where the Jew's start praying when the Egyptian army shows up and God says get moving, go and have faith. As I find myself in trouble and I know what's best to do I will pray and act with faith that things will work out.

Thank you for getting me out of some very bad situations Lord. Please help me to remain clean and serene. Amen

11/8/2011 Exodus 15:22-27, 17:1-7 – I wonder how it was that God made water come out of the rock using Moses's staff. However, this is an amazing story of God's presence, power, love, forgiveness, redemption and true care for the Jewish slaves rescued from Egypt as well as all people who love and have faith in him. I'm glad this story has been told since Moses's time until today. To me it is further proof of God and helps my faith grow.

Thank you for helping me to know you, Lord. Amen

11/9/2011 Exodus 16 – Mmmmm yum manna and quail from Heaven. I know quail tastes good but manna is described as white honey bread that forms like dew on the ground and is gathered up only as much as you need, no more or no less. Manna means "What is it" So the Jews kept on complaining and eventually got what they asked for. Meat and bread for 40 years in the wilderness. I hope God doesn't think I'm complaining like the people in this story.

Thank you for being a merciful God who listens. Please help me to trust you Lord and to have faith in all the things I do. Amen

11/10/2011 Exodus 18 – Moses had an excellent relationship with his father-in-law. They had great respect for each other and were willing to help one another in every way. I do find it difficult to talk about some things with my relatives. Generally speaking I am very blessed with the family relationships I have. As I read the Bible I am beginning to look at it with a historical perspective. 1400 BC is a long time ago with a lot of different customs, traditions, societal values and just many things I can't relate to. So slowly but surely I'm understanding how to properly relate to it.

Thanks Lord for my family and wonderful relationships. Please continue to help me grow and understand this Bible. Amen

11/11/2011 Exodus 19 – ... "Like the smoke from a brick kiln, and the whole mountain shook violently." I wonder what it would be like to see God come down on Mt. Sinai. I would probably be afraid and purify myself perfectly and be eager to witness God on the mountain.

Please help me to know you personally and closely, Lord. Thank you for helping November be an enjoyable month this year. Amen

11/12/2011 Exodus 20:1-21 – The Ten Commandments are something I've always known and sometimes followed. I do feel guilty when I break one of the rules when I'm sober enough. I do believe that if I could've followed these commandments I would not have gotten in all this trouble. Especially if I had listened to my conscience. Now that I'm clean and sober and in a relationship with Jesus I do believe as long as I follow these commandments and have Jesus, my life will be good. As well as some of the people around me that I love.

Please help me to follow your way God/Lord. Thank you for your unfailing love. Amen

11/13/2011 <u>Exodus 32</u> – Wow! God was pissed off about the Golden Calf being worshipped. Moses was almost as furious as God but he did seek forgiveness for the people.

Help me to follow your ways and thank you for Jesus and your forgiveness. Amen

11/14/2011 <u>Exodus 40</u> – Moses turned from an unsure man who didn't think he could speak well to someone that heard the Lord crystal clear and told all about Him. I believe God can and will use me for good will despite my many mistakes and weaknesses.

Lord thank you for coming into my life. Please help me to be the best I can be for you and others and me too. :) Amen

11/15/2011 <u>Numbers 12</u> – Moses sure is a blessed man! I wish I could see the Lord face to face or even in a pillar of cloud that speaks. I know what it feels like to be jealous of someone and I know it never helps to act out on those feelings. It seemed to be that all Aaron and Miriam were doing was criticizing Moses and I suppose that was not too nice, but talking about your feelings with God and someone else more calmly would've been the right thing to do.

Thank you Lord for revealing yourself to me and coming into my life. Please help me to follow your path. Amen

11/16/2011 <u>Numbers 13:1-14:4</u> – All I can do is laugh at the Jews and their complaining, I mean they bitch and moan like there's no tomorrow. In my life whining and exaggerating is something I do but it never has never really helped very much. Only if I do something about my problems head on do things get better. I'm becoming aware of God, Jesus, Holy Spirit and the power they/He has to help me in my life and others.

As I test and strengthen my faith, Lord please help me to know the real you. Thank you for helping me as much as you have, especially these last 9 months. In Jesus name Amen

11/17/2011 <u>Numbers 14:5-45</u> – God does some serious punishment for the Jews utter lack of faith after seeing countless signs and miracles. See, I wonder if there were people who felt or thought God would protect them but never spoke up and just followed the crowd in complaining and in return for not speaking up they were punished as well.

Lord help me to be brave and speak about the things that I've witnessed and gained experience from you. Thank you for your LOVE!!! Amen

11/18/2011 <u>Numbers 21:4-9</u> – These people God led out of Egypt with miracles are quick to forget God and complain about many things.

Lord please help me to go about my trials in life by remembering you, and being grateful and sincere in my repenting. Thank you for healing me as you have with my addictions and Hep C. Amen

11/19/2011 <u>Numbers 22:5-35</u> – God did an awesome job of explaining what was going to happen with Israel to Ballam and he listened. Ballam did exactly as the Lord commanded him and I believe the Lord was probably happy with him.

Lord help me to be your servant and a man who depends on your son Jesus. Thank you for your forgiveness. Amen

11/20/2011 <u>Deuteronomy 29</u> – Moses did an awesome job with God's help and started and preserved Judaism for thousands of years! I wonder if part of all the awful terrible things that have happened to the Jews are because of these covenants and promises of God?

Thank you for Jesus and the forgiveness of my sins. Please help me to be as sin free as possible and to be aware of when I do sin so that I can repent sincerely ASAP. Amen

11/21/2011 <u>Deuteronomy 30</u> – In my experience I've proven this theory to be true: Follow the ten commandments – Feel good, look good, and have nice things. Not giving a shit about God or the ten commandments – Live a totally strung out miserable, sick as hell on earth life.

Thank you for my recovery and your forgiveness. Also for showing me a new way to live. Please help me to understand LOVE. Love of you Lord and love of others. In Jesus's name. Amen

11/22/2011 <u>Deuteronomy 31:1-8</u> – So Moses and God appoint Joshua to be the next leader of Israel. I wonder how well he will do at first and how much God can change him into an amazing success like Moses.

Thank you for allowing me to be a leader in my family as the one with the most clean time. Please help me to stay strong and to give glory to you Lord. Amen

11/23/2011 <u>Deuteronomy 34</u> – Moses died at 120 years old in the area God said he would and then God buried him. What a true servant of the Lord Moses was. He saw God face to face like no other prophet has or ever will. God took a man who was unsure of his ability to speak and turned him into one of the most famous of all people that ever lived, a great leader, writer and speaker.

Thank you for reminding me that I can do great things through the Lord. You God. Please guide me. Amen

11/24/2011 <u>Joshua 1</u> – Joshua does have a lot on his shoulders, but God tells him to depend on God, and to keep doing the next right thing and all will be successful. I'm going to do my best to do this myself. I do believe it has helped me a lot so far.

Please draw me close to you Lord and thank you for your protection and forgiveness. Amen

11/25/2011 <u>Joshua 2</u> – Joshua and the walls of Jericho is a story I've heard vaguely before and I'm really enjoying it now. I wonder if Rahab and her family will be ok at the end of this story. This does reaffirm my belief that even though I've been a tweaker, heroin addict and all sorts of other bad stuff, God can still use me for good things.

Thank you for being here in me Lord, as a savior, friend, and counselor. Please help me to feel peace and to know serenity by doing the next right thing. Amen

11/26/2011 <u>Joshua 3</u> – So the Israelites use the Ark as a tool to stop the flow of the Jordan River while millions of people cross. Now that would be a sight to see. If I saw something like that 3,000 years ago I would probably be terrified.

Thank you for coming softly into my life, Lord. Please help me to show what you've done for me to others in a gentle subtle manner. Amen

11/27/2011 Joshua 5:13-6:27 – I'm happy to read that Rahab the prostitute did survive the attack of Jericho with her family. I wonder what kind of weapon the Jew's used to bring down the walls. I guess some kind of sound wave weapon. So far Joshua has been doing an awesome job of leading the Jews. I can sort of relate to Rahab because I've lived a shady couple of years and now that my faith and understanding is growing, reading a story like this does remind me that I can trust God to save me too.

Thank you for letting me back into your presence. Please help my faith and understanding continue to grow. Amen

11/28/2011 Joshua 7 – I don't like what the Jews did to Achan by stoning him and his whole family including the livestock. I just feel like that was extreme to stone his whole family and livestock. Killing him period for such a mistake might have been God's way of removing a cancer spot from the body of Israel.

Lord thank you for Jesus and your forgiveness of my terrible messed up mistakes. Please help me to understand how I can remain in your loving grace. Amen

11/29/2011 Joshua 10:1-15 – You must not murder. This is a very important commandment God gave us. So why does he tell Joshua and his army to kill every last living thing in Cannan as an offering to God? I guess the wages of sin are death and all of the people killed were guilty of one sin or another. Is there a difference between killing a person and murdering a person? Genocide of and entire region of people- men, women, kids and their animals is something I just have a hard time justifying. It's amazing what Joshua accomplished through God.

Thank you for your mercy, forgiveness and love of me and my relatives, Lord. Please help me to have you in my body, heart, mind, soul, spirit etc. and to become one with your perfect will. Amen

11/30/2011 Joshua 23 – God is dead serious about the pain and problems worshipping false idols/gods will bring upon a person back then and now, in my opinion. Now I understand why God had everything destroyed in the places his people conquered. He wanted to keep the Jewish traditions pure and for His people to not gain any new foreign god's traditions, wives etc.

Lord thank you for bringing me to you and your love and understanding. Please help me to retain and use all that I learn about you and Jesus and the Holy Spirit. Amen

12/1/2011 Joshua 24 – The people of Israel were faithful to God and no false idols for a couple of generations after Joshua. So these people took a bit to get this right but in time they came to truly know God.

Thank you for your patience and forgiveness, Lord. Please help me to be more aware of your forgiveness and patience so I can treat people around me similarly. Amen

12/2/11 Judges 4:4-24 – God does give a lot of "Tough love" in the old testament. I am starting to understand the reasoning behind all the killing and oppression but I do feel uneasy, uncertain, sad, and scared of God in these times. These are exciting books in the Bible with awesome power and very real personal relationships with God even face to face with God. I'm very grateful to be living in 2011 A.D. and not B.C. 1400.

Lord thank you for Jesus and his love and forgiveness of the terrible messed up stuff I've done. Please help me to continue to stay close in your presence and guide me to keep doing the next right thing. Amen

12/3/2011 Judges 6 – I can see how Giddeon questioned God about what He wanted him to do and to prove the angel was the Lord's angel. I would probably do the same and hopefully that would be ok. I do want to serve and obey the Lord for the remainder of my life and I'm going to do the very best I can. I do know that obeying God and following His will leads to true freedom and a good feeling like being healthy, joyous and peaceful. It satisfies me because I have felt very awful sinning and doing heroin so being clean is better than my best day all fucked up because at the end of a day I know I've done what's right in my heart. To have a clear conscience is a wonderful thing.

Thank you for Jesus and his forgiving loving Spirit. Please help me to understand the Holy Spirit too, Lord. I don't know much about it/Him? Amen

12/4/2011 Judges 13 – That's a pretty cool visual. 300 men with a burning torch in one hand and a ram's horn in the other hand yelling "A sword for the Lord and for Gideon." all of this causing chaos in a massive camp of men and camels at midnight. I like the way Gideon operates. His faith is growing and he praises God. He does God's will and makes sure it is God's will.

Thank you for your will and building my faith in you Lord. Growing closer to you feels wonderful. Please help me to know your will and the power to carry that out. Amen

12/5/2011 Judges 13 – I remember the story of Samson and how he was strong only if he never cut his hair. I do believe that as long as I walk with God I will walk strong.

Lord thank you for helping me achieve my goals and to grow closer to you. Please help me to discipline my son properly. Amen

12/6/2011 Judges 14 – Samson seems to have quite the temper and a lot of extra strength. This can be a dangerous combination to anyone that opposes him, such as the Philistines that were busy ruling over Israel. It's interesting how the Holy Spirit can cause Samson to feel, think and do certain things with great power. I wonder how many Philistines will be killed by Samson.

Thank you for Jesus and his forgiving ways, Lord. Please help me to live in your will. Amen

12/7/2011 Judges 15 – Emotions of fury, rage and revenge seem to be a big part of Samson's natural mode of operation. To me this doesn't seem to be a good, happy way to live. God used this rage to kill and start the end of the Philistine's rule over Israel.

Thank you for bringing me into your wonderful, awesome presence Lord! Please help me to keep doing the next right thing and to remain close to you forever! Amen

12/8/2011 Judges 16 – Samson was a Nazarite from birth and a man of incredible strength from God. It's really too bad that Delilah had been tempted by 1,100 pieces of Philistine silver and nagged Samson into revealing his weakness so she could give this valuable info to the Philistines. I am happy that Samson prayed for God to give him strength one last time and he accomplished his greatest feat of strength by killing thousands of Philistines in their collapsed temple.

Thank you Lord for the peaceful strength you have given me in my recovery from drugs and alcohol. Please help me to be successful, grateful and give glory to you in all I do. Amen

12/9/2011 <u>Ruth 1</u> – This book is well written. I like the way it reads so far. Ruth is one amazing friend to Naomi. I can't hardly imagine what Naomi felt like when her husband and then 2 only sons died. I wouldn't ever want to experience this sort of ordeal. Hopefully Naomi and Ruth can find peace with God and themselves.

Thank you Lord for protecting me with your grace, mercy, love and understanding forgiveness!!! Please help me to continue to grow closer and closer to you and to treat others with love like you have for me. Amen

12/10/2011 <u>Ruth 2</u> – Ruth and Naomi's story is one of amazing friendship and although it's very short I've enjoyed it immensely (a lot). It's impressive to me how much freedom and breathing room they have between them, yet at the same time they are still so close. A good friend is one of the most wonderful things a person can have. I believe finding some christian friends will do me some good.

Thank you for the relationships I still have despite my bad behavior, Lord. Please help me as I continue to seek you Lord to find some christian friends. Amen

12/11/2011 <u>Ruth 3</u> – Ruth and Naomi look out for each other with the best intentions seemingly without strings attached, and vice versa. Ruth does what Naomi suggests and everything looks like it's going to work out well for both parties.

Thank you for the relationships I can trust like Dad, Mom, Grandma and most everyone in my family Lord. Please help me to make some christian friends, Lord. Amen

12/12/2011 <u>Ruth 4</u> – All is now well for Ruth and Naomi. To think, when this story started life seemed hopeless and almost worth giving up altogether for Naomi especially. Thanks to the love of God through Ruth, Naomi and Ruth both found a happy ending. I suppose God works stuff out in his own way and we just have to do our best and trust in Him.

Thank you for your loving trustworthy embrace in my life both in times of hardships and success. Please help me to be a loving gentle yet firm father and to have better control of my anger towards Aidan. In Jesus's name Amen

12/13/2011 <u>1 Samuel 1</u> – Hannah got what she asked for and followed through with her promise to give away her only son after waiting so long to have him. This is an example of God answering a serious prayer and someone being obedient about her promises to God. She knew God was the one who made her pregnancy possible and gave her kid to God.

Thank you for keeping me out of a bunch of jail/prison time Lord and answering my prayers. Please help me to remain clean and sober and to be obedient to you. Amen

12/14/2011 <u>1 Samuel 3</u> – I'm still learning how to interact with God, Jesus and the Holy Spirit. I've become willing and ready to say "Speak, your servant is listening."

Thank you Lord for giving me a chance to be in a relationship with you because I need you. Please forgive me for the terrible things I've done and continue to help me to keep doing the next right thing. Amen

12/15/2011 <u>1 Samuel 8</u> – The Jews are in a situation where an important decision had to be made. Create a king to rule over Israel against God's warning or find a new judge. Sometimes it is hard to feel God and to know that He is real so I understand why they might've wanted a king like everybody else. I wonder how bad stuff will be in Israel after they elect this new king? I'm glad somebody was inspired by God to write all this stuff down.

Thank you Lord for showing me, a doubtful man at times, with mercy I don't deserve. Please speak to me Lord. I, your humble servant, am listening and would love to know you. Amen

12/16/2011 <u>1 Samuel 9</u> – It sounds to me like Saul is going to be a good king because God is going to be merciful on the Jews and make sure a fair man becomes King of Israel. As I read more I'm sure I'll find out. I wonder if God has anybody he speaks to today that can hear him clearly like a prophet. Also, does God still make sure the right people ultimately end up as rulers today?

Lord please help me to listen to your advice and to just do the next right thing today. Thank you for this Bible and for coming into my life. Amen

12/17/2011 <u>1 Samuel 10-12</u> – Saul is scared to be king at first. He hides by the baggage until Samuel and God go over and get him. I imagine it must've been quite a surprise for Saul to be made King.

Lord, please give me the courage to do what you have planned for me. Thank you for being here for me and my family and friends. Amen

12/18/2011 <u>1 Samuel 14</u> – Jonathan and his armor bearer did something truly amazing by faith in God and his ability to do anything. Saul is another example of an imperfect ruler God used to achieve what needed to be done.

Please help me to know you Lord and to be in your presence. Thank you for the love and forgiveness and power of a relationship with you that I have found so far God, Jesus and Holy Spirit. Amen

12/19/2011 <u>1 Samuel 17:1-38</u> – David believes so strongly that God can defeat Goliath - this terrifying giant warrior - that he goes ahead and decides to fight all by himself. The most interesting thing is that he doesn't do it for the reward but to defend God's honor and to show His power to do anything.

Thank you for the powerful feeling I had about Jesus last night, Lord. It means the world to me. To know you and do right by you is what I ultimately want. Please continue to be with me and help grow my faith. Amen

12/20/2011 <u>1 Samuel</u> – Samuel is getting old by now I'd think. David and Saul get along wonderfully even though David has secretly been anointed as King to be. David chose to respect and take good care of Saul despite all the stuff between them. It's interesting that David looks like a small young un-kingly guy, but God ends up being right about the fact that David will be Israel's greatest king of all.

Please help me to be respectful to my elders/authorities/society and to always contribute with a good attitude to the best of my ability. Thank you for healing me of so much poison and bad bad choices Lord. Amen

12/21/2011 1 Samuel 17:38-58 – David kills Goliath who is between 6.75 feet and over 9 feet tall and has been a man of war since youth. David hit Goliath in the forehead hard with a rock thrown by a sling. First shot. This knocks the big guy down and out a little. David then jumps up on top of him, pulls out Goliath's own sword and beheads the large man. David does all this in the name of the living God of Israel with more courage and faith than I can hardly imagine.

Please help me to at least tell people I'm a christian and how well things have become for me because of this. Thank you for helping me to find my way to you and your love, peace, joy, serenity, courage, satisfaction and pure awesomeness of your presence in my life Lord. Amen

12/22/2011 1 Samuel 18 – Saul appears to be the only person that intends to harm David. I believe jealousy can cause this sort of reaction towards friends, family, coworkers, etc. The trick for me is to pray for that person's success and to ask that God's will be fulfilled in their life. Sometimes it's hard to do but praying helps me to accept what's going on around me and to just try my best to achieve my own goals.

Thank you Lord for coming into my life and giving the power of surrender to your will and acceptance of reality. Please help me to be in your will/plan for me as I try my best to reach for my dreams. Amen

12/23/2011 1 Samuel 19, 20 – Saul has become completely psycho, throwing spears at David and his son. Partly because of the evil spirit, but mostly out of hate and jealousy I think. Jonathan and David's relationship is based around their same beliefs about Judaism. What a loyal friendship though.

Please help me to be courageous and at peace today as I go about my day. Thank you for the good relationships I have in my life today. In Jesus name Amen

12/24/2011 <u>1 Samuel 24</u> "From evil people come evil deeds." How true but it can be hard to repay evil with good instead of fighting fire with more fire.

Thank you for keeping me out of jail/prison and for my health and happiness and for the well being of the ones I love, Lord. Please help me and my family to have a safe, happy and satisfying Christmas. Amen

12/25/2011 <u>1 Samuel 25-26</u> – The story of David is truly an engaging one. I find real deepness to the characters and plot line. David is a good man, and I love reading about his relationship with God and the things God does for/around David.

Thank you from the bottom of my heart for a wonderful Christmas and for being in my life these days God, Jesus and Holy Spirit. Please continue to guide me in your way. Amen

12/26/2011 <u>1 Samuel 28:31</u> – Saul goes to a medium and she truly can talk to the spirit of dead Samuel. Samuel tells Saul exactly what's going to happen next too. The philistines kill Saul and his sons and the army runs off and some die too.

Please help me to be softer and gentler with firm and effective yet patient loving care of Aidan, my only son, Lord. Thank you for my freedom and sobriety today. In Jesus name Amen

12/27/2011 <u>2 Samuel 1-5</u> – David can be very quick to kill. I don't agree with the way he killed the Amalekite messenger at Ziklag. I do love the relationship he has with God and the deep respect for people he loves and knows.

Lord, please help me to seek you in all things. Thank you for coming into my life with all the peace, comfort and guidance of your Spirit and loving, forgiving son Jesus. Amen!

12/28/2011 <u>2 Samuel 6, 7, 9, 10</u> – David was very blessed in his military campaigns. When the Ark killed Uzzah, I can relate with the fear, hurt and confusion David felt towards the Holy Ark of God. I love the way David treats Jonathan's crippled son Mephibosheth. He gives him property and respect.

Please help me to know you and your will Lord. Thank you for your loving forgiving son Jesus Christ in my life. Amen

12/29/2011 <u>2 Samuel 11</u> – David is human after all. He was overcome with the sheer beauty of a woman, got her pregnant and tried to cover that up. He couldn't get her husband to sleep with her so he killed him and then married her. Wow. You know the Bible is full of wonderful real messages.

Please help me to follow your will for me and to obey your very wonderful commandments, Lord. Thank you for showing me such vast amounts of mercy, Lord. amen

12/30/2011 <u>2 Samuel 12</u> – So David's punishment for this nasty crime/sin against God is that his newborn child dies and his family will rebel against him and he will live by the sword. At least God decides to continue to be in contact and in relationship with David. I'm sure David is very glad about this and will continue on and do his very best in the name of the Living God of Israel.

Lord, please help me to do what's right to remain in a healthy relationship with you and therefore others. Thank you God for being in my life and keeping me safe, happy, healthy, free and so so many more wonderful things today. Amen

12/31/2011 <u>2 Samuel 13:1-22</u> – The bible is full of some stories that upset me, but this one is probably one of the very worst. To rape his own half sister, then toss her away with hate and disgust. He could've just married her. I mean come on. For fuck's sake man. I hope as I read on that justice can be done for all parties involved, <u>as God sees fit</u>. Key words being as God sees fit.

Please help me to turn to you more and more in all areas of my life. Thank you for the grace and amazing mercy you have shown me Lord. In Jesus name, Amen

1/1/2012 <u>2 Samuel 13:23-39, 14</u> – Absalom held his grudge for quite some time. He waited two years for the moment to kill Amnon. Then 3 years away from his father and Israel, and another 2 years before seeing and talking to King David, his dad. I don't think any part of that whole situation was in any way righteous. I can only imagine what it would be like to feel the pain of anyone of these peoples perspectives.

Please help me to turn to you Lord when I find myself in times of extreme feelings and suffering. Thank you for the Holy Spirit and what Christ has done for me especially in 2011. Amen

1/2/2012 <u>2 Samuel 15, 16, 17</u> – Absalom is one seriously vengeful and talented young man. It's too bad he put all of that energy in stuff that doesn't seem right to me from a 3rd party perspective hindsight view. David is a truly blessed man. He lets God guide him in all that he did and thought of others as well.

Please give me the right decision on what I should do with my opportunity to take a study class on Christianity Lord. Thank you for another peaceful and successful day sober. Amen

1/3/2012 <u>2 Samuel 18, 19</u> – Joab does have a good point in some of the stuff he does but he is a murderous bastard. David should've never slept with Bathsheba and killed her husband Uriah the Hittite, because his family most definitely rebelled against him. It's nice he could rely on God and still do his best through God even after his mistakes.

Please let your will be done in my own life and those of the ones I love around me Lord. Let us sleep well and the house showing go as it needs to. Thank you for a nice safe place for me and my family to live and love. Amen

1/4/2012 <u>1 Kings 1</u> – I read a good bit of the end of 2 Samuel also, and this is all a lot to take in. I think it's interesting that God, David, and Nathan wanted Solomon to be King instead of the next oldest son of David. Solomon was a result of David's sinful lust with Bathsheba. Also, Solomon had 700 wives and 300 concubines!!! WOW!!! How did that work out? That just doesn't seem wise to me. Anyway I look forward to reading on.

Please help me to lean on and grow as close as I can to you Lord. Thank you for all the love and protection you've blessed me and my family with. In Jesus name. Amen

1/5/2012 <u>1 Kings 2,3,4:1-20</u> – So Solomon got his wisdom by asking God in prayer and sacrifice, then in a dream. For such an awesome power, he only had to choose to follow God's laws and asked God. David's last words were short and sweet to his son Solomon. It seems like Joab and everybody else all got what they asked for. I wonder what other very interesting stuff I'll read about next?

Please help me get over my jealousy of others and to pray for them as well as my enemies and equals. Thank you so very much for your presence in my life, Lord. I love your guiding, loving, good feeling ways through Jesus. In Jesus name. Amen

1/6/2012 <u>1 Kings 5, 6, part of 7</u> – What an awesome temple for God Solomon built.

Lord please watch over my sister Roxann, and give her the right decision for her relationship with Ryan. Please keep her close to you and protect her from harm. Especially drugs and alcohol. Thank you so much for all the peace and happiness and safety and love and forgiveness you have shown me and my family. Amen

1/7/2012 <u>1 Kings 9, 10 and most of 11</u> – So Solomon's downfall was his 700 royal wives and 300 concubines. They led him to build altars to other gods and to forget about GOD. His accomplishments are truly amazing and the amount of mercy God showed him is equally awesome.

Please help me to stay close to Christ and your laws, Lord because I know they are the right thing to do. Thank you for me and my sister's sobriety today. Amen

1/8/2012 <u>1 Kings Rest or 11, 12, 13</u> – I feel unsure of my decision to go and take this class on Sundays for 16 weeks about Jesus and the Bible. I just don't want to be misled or brainwashed, or forced into doing stuff I don't want to do or think.

Please help me to know/feel whether what I'm doing is right or wrong Lord. And to keep the pull of evil and unjustified fear at bay. Thank you for giving me the courage to face my fears today with you in my life, prayers, and thoughts. Amen

1/9/2012 <u>1 Kings 17</u> – Elijah was fed by ravens and drank water from a brook for some time. How fascinating, I had no idea God could even do such amazing things and that someone recorded the story. He also was fed by a widow and her dying son from a never ending flour and oil bowl until the drought ended and the widow found more food. Also, bringing a dead boy back to life! Wow how cool a story this is I read today. I believe this, mostly because I'm really feeling it and how could you make this stuff up?

Please help me to have the proper attitude and to curb my lying when getting into my ego driven arguments with dad, Lord. Thank you for your love and way of living that has brought me great peace through good behavior and trust in you Lord. In Jesus name Amen

1/10/2012 <u>1 Kings 18</u> – Elijah had all the prophets of Baal killed after they could not perform their miracle. All 400 of them. Eye for and eye and tooth for a tooth seems to be a recurring theme in the old testament. It is amazing that he could pray for rain after 3 years of drought and then run faster than a horse and chariot.

Please help me to worship you Lord and not any other idols. Thank you for Jesus and his teaching of kindness and forgiveness. Amen

1/11/2012 <u>1 Kings 19, 20</u> – God has always been a gentle whisper in my life. Never anything dramatic and I'm thankful that nothing scary either. I read some stuff in Galatians today also and I have an answer to my prayer about this weekend. I have faith in Christ and don't need to follow rules about going to study the Bible to find salvation.

Thank you Lord for answering my prayers with the Bible and for doing it in a subtle way I could meditate on. Please watch over Aidan while he is with Cynthia. Amen

1/12/2012 <u>1 Kings 21</u> – It's too bad Naboth got in the way of Ahab's lustful jealous desire for the vineyard of Naboth's ancestors. Jezebel has been one truly evil, conniving, hateful, vengeful God awful influence on Ahab and his behavior. I'm surprised and happy to see that Ahab was humble and scared of God and especially that God showed mercy on him despite his many many offenses. Ahab's whole story goes to show the influence a bad woman or other person can have on you.

Please help me to know who is good for me in the long or short run and how to have healthy relationships with all the people around me Lord. Thank you for the miracle of recovery you have given me and my family. Thank you so so much for the loving and wise parents that Roxann and I have. Amen

1/13/2012 <u>1 Kings 22</u> – King Ahab didn't listen to bad advice from wise counsel and everything turned out exactly like the prophet said it would. Who or what is this Baal people were worshipping back in those days? In my own time people still do the same stuff they did back then. Ahab died, but I wonder what happened to the prophet he put in jail for giving him an answer he did not want to hear? I wonder what is going to happen in 2 Kings?

1/14/2012 <u>2 Kings 1, 2:1-12</u> – Elijah the confronter and Elisha the comforter. Some truly miraculous things Elijah has done and it seems Elisha will be 2X the spirit of Elijah. The Bible is an exciting and entertaining book. Full of character building wisdom for the ages.

Lord, please help things to go well with Cynthia and Aidan. Please make sure they are safe, happy and healthy. Thank you for the awesome love, support, gifts of my Mom and Grandma. Amen

1/15/2012 <u>2 Kings 2:13-25, 3, 4</u> – Wow Elisha has performed some truly amazing miracles through the Lord. I want to grow in my faith and such. I'm just having a hard time with being grateful for what I have.

Please help me to do the right thing and be humble and a grateful person Lord. Thank you for watching over my son and for a nice warm bed for us to sleep in. Amen

1/16/2012 <u>2 Kings 5, 6, 7, 8, 9, 10</u> – Elisha performed many amazing miracles. There was a lot of killing going on back then also.

Please help me to have the right attitude towards Dad and his "Stuff" Lord. Please help me to keep my anger in check and to do and say the right thing. Thank you for Mom and the love of my family on my birthday. Amen

1/17/2012 <u>2 Kings 11, 12, 13 mostly</u> – It's my 23rd birthday today.

Joash did a good job thanks to his wise counsel from his adopted father, priest Jehoiada and the other priests in the Lord's temple. Similar to Elisha's last prophecy though, he needed to show more enthusiasm for God as well as showing his ability to follow wise instruction.

Thank you for a truly wonderful birthday with my family and happy, healthy sobriety!! Please stay with me during this year and let me grow closer to you Lord every day!! Amen

1/18/2012 <u>2 Kings 18, 19, 20. 22, 23</u> – Hezekiah and Josiah were the only "good" kings mentioned in 2 Kings. Josiah followed God passionately with his body, mind, soul and most importantly with lots of action.

Please help me to have a close and deep connection with you Jesus my Lord and savior. Thank you for letting things work out so well in my life and my family's life today. Amen

1/19/2012 <u>Ezra 3</u> – The temple meant the world to these now free Jews trying to rebuild their lives with God. They spent months just preparing and cried/shouted for joy when the foundation had finally been laid.

Lord, please help me to grow closer and closer to you everyday and to always have you in my life. Thank you for the peace of mind and body you've brought me and my family. Amen

1/20/2012 <u>Nehemiah 2</u> – I wonder if this is when Jerusalem is rebuilt all the way? It's a bold and awesome plan Nehemiah has to rebuild his ancestors' home.

Please help things to turn around with my driving privileges Lord and to be patient as I try to work towards my goals ultimately letting you Lord direct my life/will through the Holy Spirit. Thank you for the healing peace-giving presence you have had in my life. Amen

1/21/2012 <u>Nehemiah 5</u> – Not charging interest? That sounds so strange yet proper when talking about family and friends. For a governor to not use as much of his financial budget as possible. Wow! Nehemiah was a good dude.

Please help me to control my reaction and to have a good relationship with my dad. Thank you for the opportunity to get to know the Bible tomorrow. Amen

1/22/12 <u>Nehemiah 8</u> – My first INSTE class was just an introduction but it did go well today. Nehemiah did begin to rebuild Jerusalem physically and Spiritually. I don't know who I will live with next or how I will go to school and if I will drive a car again. Maybe I would rather go to school and live with Mom right now in her house with Jesse, Jessica, Roxann and Aidan. I guess I'll do what needs to be done for Aidan until I can get a clear idea of what to do with my living situation.

Please help things to go according to your will Lord and to help me achieve my goals. Thank you for an awesome birthday party tonight with my family! Amen

1/23/2012 <u>Esther 1</u> – King Xerxes threw a party that lasted for 180 days of unlimited wine and food!! That's what I call overboard but still kinda cool. Then he had his beautiful wife banished because she didn't obey his one command to come out and show off to the nobleman. Things were different between men and women back then and now in the middle east.

Thank you for my awesome opportunities and abilities being born in America Lord. Please help me to have strong faith in Jesus tonight and to fill me with your Holy Spirit Lord. Amen

1/24/2012 <u>Esther 2</u> – Esther is a Cinderella type story and very fascinating so far. Hadassah is Esther's name and the name of my Mom's employer's salon.

Lord please let the house sell if it is your will and help me to find a new safe place to live. Thank you for the opportunity I have to start going to church. Amen

1/25/2012 <u>Esther 3</u> – My teeth hurt too bad yesterday night to even write. I did read and pray for relief and took a bunch of Advil and Tylenol to feel better.

Thank you for helping me to feel better, Lord. Amen

1/26/2012 <u>Esther 4</u> – Mordecai kind of caused this but I can understand why he refused to bow down to that A-hole Haman. I imagine it was truly frightening for Esther to have to go before the king and die just for not being invited. I can truly admire her attitude of fasting about it. Time to think and then she says, "If I must die, I must die."

Thank you for the courage and sense of peace your presence has brought into my life, Lord. Please help me keep you close to my heart, body and spirit, Lord. Amen

1/27/12 <u>Esther 5</u> – Everything is going well so far. The king held out his gold scepter and accepted Esther's presence in his inner court with the reply "What do you want... I will give it to you, even if it is half the kingdom." So her fear was well placed and strong but everything worked out very well so far.

Lord, please help me to remain grateful and to stay close to you. Thank you for the peace and courage you have given me today. Amen

1/28/12 Esther 6, 7, 8, 9, 10 – What a good ending to a very enjoyable book to read. Esther's bravery truly paid off and her people were saved. (Jews) Haman and his sons were impaled in their own courtyard. King Xerxes was a fair and just king in the end too. God may not be mentioned directly in this book but He is definitely part of the plan and ending to this story.

Lord, please help me to find peace and to be grateful for all that I have. Thank you for my opportunity to go to church tomorrow and get a feel for this kind of fellowship. Amen

1/29/12 Job 1 – Wow!!! All his children died and animals died or were captured in an instant. And almost all his servants were killed too. "Satan the Accuser" was allowed to test Job and boy did he. I wonder what the "Members of the Heavenly court" and "Sons of God" were exactly? And after all this he still did not blame God. "The Lord gave me what I had, and the Lord has taken it away." How brave and true a statement to make in an insane moment of pain.

Lord, thank you for a good day at church and for helping me to control my reaction to the world around me. Please help watch over Roxann and keep her clean and sober. Also, heal David of his sickness. Amen

1/30/12 Job 2, 3 and bits and pieces until 38 – Boils from head to toe just to top it off! I could imagine this would be enough to cause a man like Job to curse his very existence. This is a very interesting book though. I always thought I would like it, even before I knew what it was about. I guess there is room for growth in my pains and disappointments.

Lord, please help me to be brave and remain grateful in the grips of my pain and struggles. Thank you so very much for the vast mercy and sweet life I have with Jesus. Amen

1/31/12 Job 38, 39, 40, 41 – I wonder if the creatures God is talking about, "Behemoth and Leviathan" were ever real. The Leviathan sounds like a badass Dragon. God probably had a good reason for letting Satan test Job. I can understand God's explanation as appropriate and Job's reaction seems humanly normal.

Please help things to go well tomorrow and if it's your will Lord, help me to drive again and go to school with Aidan in preschool. Thank you for your loving merciful presence and another wonderful day. Amen

2/1/2012 Job 42 – So ends another intriguing book in this Bible of mine. After all of Job's tests and amazingly painful disaster, God spoke to and appeared in front of Job's eyes with only questions to answer for Job's outcry of angry, upset and sad questions. Job was a good man and repented for his bad attitude against the Lord God. He was also humble enough to forgive his ignorant friends and pray for them on God's behalf for the things they had said and done. In the end God helped Job to gain 2X the rich life he had before the catastrophe.

Lord, Thank you for letting my motorcycle title show up!!! Please help me to grow in my spiritual maturity and to be a good disciple of Jesus Christ. Amen

2/2/2012 Psalm 1 – Do I want to be successful in all I do, have joy, and delight in the law of the Lord meditating on it day and night? I most definitely do! I've tried not giving a shit and going down a very very self-destructive path and it is hell on earth having to be sick with sin and disease day in and day out. I love my newfound relationship with the Lord. I don't care what anybody says, even my dad is a discouraging person. I know he's just looking out for me.

Lord, I love you and your presence in my life! Please help me to be more like Jesus and to keep your word deep in my heart! Thank you for the many awesome miracles you have performed in my life. I am a truly, truly blessed man. I am sorry for my bad attitude at times and the awful things I've done. Amen

2/3/2012 <u>Psalm 5, 8</u> – I know I have worth because people around me tell me I do, and I read that I have worth to God despite my many flaws. This does make me feel good, acceptable and worthy of life, love and happiness. For a while I didn't think I needed God in my life, and it is so nice to now know that I ABSOLUTELY do NEED God in my life.

Please watch over me and my family Lord and help me to obey you and to know you closely. Thank you for coming into my life and giving so many miraculous blessings! Amen Luv you!

2/4/2012 <u>Psalm 15, 23, 25</u> – Psalm 23 "He lets me rest in green meadows, He leads me beside peaceful streams." That is the most comforting phrase in Psalm 23. This whole Psalm is very comforting. I feel like it is a true treasure to be able to read about it today.

Please help me to be productive and hear what is best for me tomorrow, Lord. Thank you for protecting me and my family through our many mistakes. Amen

2/5/2012 <u>Psalm 51</u> – My actions show my sorrow over the wrong choices I made by the way I have changed. The things that hurt are often wrong and cause me to feel immense sorrow when I realize what I've done. It does feel good, really good to have Jesus to pray to and to know that he loves me, will help me to change and forgive my incredible mistakes.

Please help me to stay on the righteous path Lord. Thank you for another wonderful day with you in my life as Captain. Amen

2/6/2012 <u>Psalms 103, 104</u> – Psalm 103:9, "He will not constantly accuse us, nor remain angry forever." This is the part of Psalm 103 that helps me to better understand God. I know I am making lots of mistakes and I'm glad to know now that God doesn't want to accuse me and stay mad. He wants to forgive me and help me to obey His laws.

Lord, please help me to stay close to you and to keep learning what you can teach me. Thank you for the strength and good health you have blessed me with today. Amen

2/7/2012 <u>Psalms 139</u> – When I read this Psalm I feel loved and reassured that God is close to me and knows me intimately. I'm comforted to know God has a plan for me. My favorite part of 139:7 "I can never escape from your Spirit! I can never get away from your presence!"

Lord, thank you for always being with me and for the love and strength you have given me. Please help me to follow your laws and lead me along the path of everlasting life. Amen

2/8/2012 <u>Psalms 145</u> – I most need God's ability to help those who have fallen and ask for help. They need help after making big mistakes. 145:14 "The Lord helps the fallen and lifts those bent beneath their loads."

Lord please help my Aunt Leesa, Grandma, Grandpa, cousins Justin and Mike, Marc Norris, Emily, Samantha, Roxann and anyone else hurt by Leesa's actions. (She got charged with theft and trafficking.) Please bring them peace and comfort in their time of great stress. Please bless them and make them strong. Please bring them to you, Jesus and to others who have been through similar things. Thank you for your mercy and the miracle you've worked in my life. Amen

2/9/2012 Proverbs 4 – Finding wisdom is something I'm scared to ask God for. I've heard it can involve great trials and tribulation. In my experience, tough times do increase wisdom by necessity. I am afraid of going through pain and suffering. I guess I do want wisdom and for sure to stay on the righteous path. Good judgement is also a priority for me because I know how important that is.

If it is your will, Lord please grant me wisdom and good judgement. Thank you for being near me today and forever. Amen

2/10/2012 Proverbs 5 – These are wise words about sex and healthy happy relationships with a woman and or a wife. Unfortunately this is the complete opposite of what I see on TV, magazines, movies, (sometimes), billboards and many people I've been around. I want to practice self control and find a wife someday. It's just that I'm scared of most women and the pain that can come from the feelings I have for them. Finding a great wife is the dream of most men I believe.

Lord, please help me to have self control and to be a moral man. Please guide me and lead me down the path you have planned for me with Jesus and the Holy Spirit. Thank you for coming into my life and being my savior and King. Amen

2/11/2012 Ecclesiastes 1-12 – Sad but true statements by Solomon in this book. Life is meaningless without God and an afterlife. Today I can remember my creator by reading the Bible, going to church, AA/NA, prayer, meditation and by talking about God with friends, family and any people or watching TV, internet, movies, magazines and books. To keep

God in my mind I center my thinking and behavior more and more around God, Jesus and the Holy Spirit.

Lord, please help me to grow ever closer to you and to stay on the righteous path. Thank you for another wonderful day and for your love and care. Amen

2/12/12 Isaiah 6 – I can relate to Isaiah's feelings at first in awe of God, then fear, guilt, gratitude for his forgiveness, and then an eagerness to go and do for the Lord what he asked. For my many sins and mistakes I feel very sad and guilty. To express my need for forgiveness, I cried and prayed to God to forgive me and to let Jesus come into my heart, life and my whole being guiding me henceforth.

Lord, please help the people in my life that need you and your love and protection most. Thank you for your constant presence in my life. Amen

2/13/2012 Isaiah 53 – I would describe what Jesus did for me as an act of such deep and profound meaningful loving service that I am going to spend my time trying to understand who and what He is all about. I'm at a loss for words to describe what Jesus did for me.

Lord, thank you for Jesus and for taking my sins and the sin of the whole world. Please help me to stay on the righteous path you intend for me. I love you. Amen

2/14/2012 Jeremiah 1 – Sober and clean Valentines Day!! If I were Jeremiah I probably would have felt scared and cautious to accept God's command but with time and thought I would've done the best I could to be God's go to guy. I think God wants me to help people and to spread his message about my miraculous recovery and life change. I think God wants me to be the best father and person to all the people I meet and to be brave when speaking in public.

Lord, please help me to get to Nicaragua for the mission's trip with my grandpa, and to be a brave good speaking Addict/Alcoholic. Thank you for protecting Aidan while he was with his mom. Amen Happy Valentine's Day I love you.

2/15/2012 Jeremiah 36 – In my relationship with the Lord the risks I take are being influenced by false teachers and saying something that would piss somebody off. I am very fortunate to not have too many dangers involved in my walk with God.

Lord, please watch over me and my family and make sure I learn the proper teaching of your Word. Thank you for the wonderful happy peaceful life I have today. Amen

2/16/12 Jeremiah 38 – The only part of my life that compares to Jeremiah being down in the well is when I was in jail. Dad and mom were the only ones who came to bail me out. Jeremiah was doing the right thing and got punished whereas I was deserving of jail for the most part. I was stuck in the mud and loneliness of my bad decisions knowing I may die if I had kept up with the drugs and alcohol. I feel Christ came to my rescue in a long term plan to save my soul too.

Lord, please lead me and keep me in line with your will. Thank you for another easy peaceful day with my son. Amen

2/17/12 Ezekiel 37:1-14 – I have most certainly been spiritually dry, dead, and bankrupt. When doing heroin, meth, cocaine, alcohol, pot, tobacco etc. I was a criminally insane asshole who had no God and hated myself and others. I've done my best to turn my life around this past year and I'm so glad I have a God/Savior/guiding Spirit. I owe a debt of gratitude to the people that brought this wonderful info that has changed my life.

Lord, please help me to show my gratitude by helping other lost spiritually dead people. Thank you for saving me. Amen

2/18/12 Daniel 1 – I usually respond to group/peer pressure with fearful conformation to the social norms of the people around me at the time. If something can be done about it I will try to change things and keep my true feelings and beliefs inside me. When somebody else speaks up is usually when I will agree with them so that way I don't feel like an outcast.

Lord, please give me the strength to hold on to what is righteous under all situations. Thank you Lord for another wonderful day and for your ever present presence in my life. Amen

2/19/12 Daniel 2:1-24 – Seemingly hopeless situations bring out qualities in me like: fear, **DESPERATION**, depression, anger, worry, hate, confusion, panic, sadness, energy, racing thoughts, insomnia and eventually a desire to find a solution and to carry on and never forget what brought me there and how I can avoid it. I think a hopeless situation brings this out in me because I want things to go a certain way and not to be hurt or feel pain. I need to work on accepting things as they are, do my best and leave the rest to GOD.

Lord, please help me to learn to depend on you. Thank you for another awesome day with my family. Amen

2/20/12 Daniel 2:25-49 – When things go right in my life as of late, I give the credit to the people who helped me, God, and the things that I did to make it happen. I give credit to these people and God because I know it makes me feel good when people honor me and I'm grateful for things going the right way. I also want to teach others how I succeeded.

Lord, please help me to give credit where credit is due, properly. Thank you for another perfect day with you Lord. Amen

2/21/12 <u>Daniel 3</u> – Examples of God's protection in my life are: protecting my unborn son while he was in the womb when me and his mom were doing heroin and whatever else, curing my Hep C, keeping me out of prison and or more jail time. My sobriety is almost a year long, just to have lived and recovered from my very large mistakes. Ultimately God has protected me from going down the path of destruction alone and dying without a God.

Lord, thank you for coming into my life and for always looking out for me. Please help me to do what's right and to never stray from your love again. Amen

2/22/12 <u>Daniel 4,5</u> – I think the message God has for our society is found in the Bible and inside of those people that look for God in their lives. I don't know that much about God, but I do know that the more I learn about God, Jesus and the Holy Spirit, the more I feel spiritually in touch with God and the universe. I think the truth is out there and if you search you will find.

Lord, please show me the truth of your power and existence, keep me close to you and on the right track. Thank you for coming into my life and bringing me peace. Amen

2/23/12 <u>Daniel 6</u> – My hand hurts from so much writing lately. Great story about Daniel and the lions.

Please help me to continue to stay close to you Lord and to spend time with you. Thank you for another clean and happy day. Amen

18
Closing thoughts from Konrad

I have come so far after my AVM. I truly believe I had a miracle. My AVM could have happened any day since I was born. I believe we all have destinies. I believe God loves us all. A human being will die someday so I will find moments of love as long as I am alive.

Everything is weak and slow on the right side of my body. My barriers are in my brain that affected my language. This deficit is called aphasia. I do not always understand everything and I can't speak correctly. Two years after my stroke I asked Cindy and Jake if Aidan could live with me and they said no. Aidan was going into 1st grade. But then they broke up and Aidan moved in with us.

Looking back my progress has been slow but I have come so far! I am not a normal human being. Having a massive brain bleed is very serious. I can communicate and comprehend better and better. Repetitive definitions on my phone for words I don't know while I am reading helps a lot.

I can only imagine becoming a sad person who had a stroke. We all have trials and tribulations. I am so grateful for where I am living.

I will never forget those times when I helped serve, cook, and do dishes at the Share Homestead. Helping needy people feels good.

I do believe that having an AVM brain bleed on February 24th, 2012, exactly one year after getting clean and sober is not a coincidence. God works in mysterious ways. God set a plan for my life. I will die someday so I am treasuring every last moment of life's ups and downs.

I am still reading my Bible on Sunday mornings and writing in my journal. I was doing this 7 days a week but my routine changed about 2 years ago when I started working with a physical therapist again to try to correct my gait. She has given me many exercises to do.

Now, after my hip fracture I am working with the same PT as I did right after my stroke 13 years ago. Soon I will be back to work. The hip surgery has been very painful but I will recover. I am very grateful for Kaiser and Rebound Orthopedics, and all the other surgeons and doctors that have helped me. My right leg is now 2 inches shorter than my left leg. We are trying to get some shoes specially adapted to help with that.

Aidan is the one I love the strongest. I am always thinking about him. Our families taught us to love each other. Love is the very strongest of all.

I am a survivor. Losing loved ones is very sad. All things will pass. Grief is different for everyone. The pain never goes away completely. There are so many people who have had strokes, cancer and heart attacks in my country. I have met many people that have suffered an AVM. Some were sad and some were crippled. The doctor wasn't sure how the stroke would affect me long term. I was unable to even talk until my brain started connecting again. I am a miracle. My recovery has been miraculous.

I very rarely watch television after my stroke, but I still love reading books.

I will never give up. I love sharing my hope and perseverance with people. Give and receive. I will continue paying back for what I have done. There are good and bad memories of before my stroke that I will never forget. There is so much that was erased from my memory. My sister, mom and dad have shown me pictures from when I was a kid. I have said this many times, it is amazing that I have regained my brain and other parts of my body. I am thankful for Marshall Community Center so I can keep strengthening my body. I love seeing and talking to people there.

Aidan took swim lessons at Marshall Community Center. He loves to swim. He has lots of energy. Aidan must have perseverance of his own. He has experienced many traumas in his life already.

When my mom and dad got divorced that was very sad. I was using drugs and was starving for my heroin at that time. Drugs can cause so many problems. Marijuana was the first drug I used. Drugs and alcohol can destroy a person's life.

Using CVan and my bicycle has helped give me a sense of independence. I still love volunteering with the Summer Meals Program for needy families. Luckily my hip has healed enough to volunteer again this summer.

No matter what, never give up!

19

Community

Trust God to fill you so you can pour out to others.

Psalm 46:1 states:

"God is our refuge and strength, a very present help in times of trouble."

This verse emphasizes God's role as a source of safety, power and immediate assistance during difficult times. It assures believers that they can find refuge in God's presence and strength when facing adversity.

Philippians 4:13

"I can do all things through Christ who strengthens me."

This is a good verse to memorize, to remind yourself during difficult times that we can do hard things! Apostle Paul wrote this verse in prison. Believers have the ability to find contentment and strength in Christ no matter what. A relationship with Jesus is a promise of unconditional love and spiritual support through the good times and the bad times. We are not alone. We are created to live in community with other people so we can help each other. Praying with others is very powerful. Sharing our cares with others is a very intimate thing to do. Be brave and trust God. Encourage others with love.

Nehemiah 8:10

"The joy of the Lord is my strength."

- Source of strength, this verse suggests that the joy derived from God is not just a fleeting emotion, but a powerful source of strength and stability. This joy is rooted in God's faithfulness and goodness, providing a foundation for enduring challenges.

- Overcoming adversity with the "Joy of the Lord" can help believers to persevere and find strength in their faith. It can help maintain a positive outlook and focus on God's promises no matter how bleak and painful the circumstances are.

- Rejoicing amidst suffering is possible. You can experience joy even in the season of suffering and hardship. This joy is not a denial of pain but a recognition of God's presence and love.

- Spiritual and emotional well being is found in the "Joy of the Lord". It delivers peace, hope and contentment while navigating life's greatest challenges.

Inspiration and motivation in the "Joy of the Lord" honors God and inspires believers to serve others. Be filled with God's joy so you can pour out God's love to others to build them up. Loving others is the reason for our faith and hope.

Chances are good that if you're not going through something challenging now you probably just went through something or are about to go through something. Following Jesus doesn't mean life will be a piece of cake. He promised that there will be trials and tribulation but that we would never be alone through it all. Jesus loves us enough to not leave us just as He finds us.

We need accountability. Gather with others to edify and build one another up. Be willing to be authentic with someone you can trust and pray for each other, lifting one another up in love.

AA and NA 12-step programs are designed to help people look at their character defects and start the process of healing so that you can keep what you have by giving it away. Ideally you don't ever quit AA or NA once you are FREE. You have a sponsor to work the steps with, and then you work the steps with other suffering addicts and alcoholics for as long as you're physically able.

As you grow in faith as a believer, God brings to your attention the pride, fears, shame, guilt, hate, anger and other issues that may be keeping you from fulfilling your God given destiny. Jesus is in the business of healing and restoration. Lay your burdens at the foot of the cross and surrender your will and follow his teachings of love and forgiveness. Jesus died a gruesome death on that cross so that all our sins can be forgiven and we can have His JOY. Say thank you often.

Following Jesus is a never ending process of working through character flaws as we are ready to face them. Relax and talk to God as you would a trusted friend. Invite Jesus into your heart and discover the awesome power of His Great Love! Then go shine that light and love in the deep dark places and be amazed and filled with awe, delight and joy. We do not have to go through anything alone and be chronically empty inside. Jesus loves you more than you can imagine. Seek Jesus and the Kingdom of God, keep seeking, never stop seeking. Pray and build a relationship with Him and never stop praying. Forgive as you have been forgiven. Be the light in someone else's storm. Be still and listen to that voice inside you. Be thankful. Develop an attitude of gratitude. We are in control of 90% of how we respond to what happens to us. Be thankful in all circumstances. Keep on being thankful! I'm not OK and you're not OK but Jesus loves us anyway.

Miracle: Supernatural Phenomenon

- A highly improbable or extraordinary event, development or accomplishment that brings very welcome consequences.

- A surprising and welcome event that can't be explained by nature or scientific laws, and is therefore considered to be the work of a divine agency.

Joy: The true definition of Joy goes beyond the limited explanation presented in a dictionary – "A feeling of great pleasure and happiness." True joy is limitless, life defining, a transformative reservoir waiting to be tapped into. It requires the utmost surrender, and like love, is a choice to be made.

The difference that prayer and faith make in suffering hardships makes all the difference. It is wonderful when you know that another prayer has been answered. God works through community, and our purpose will always be to love even the unlovable and to encourage each other. Keep on loving even when it seems impossible.

Closing prayer:

Heavenly Father, I pray each person reading this will find, follow and fulfill your will for their life. I pray they experience the awesome power of your great love, amazing grace and JOY! In Jesus's name Amen

By the way, that friend of mine who hadn't seen or heard from her son in five months, found him on Facebook so at least she knows that he is still alive.

Don't quit 5 minutes before your miracle!

Never give up! Anything is possible!

Thank you for reading this book about Konrad's healing journey. If you would like to contact Konrad for any reason, here is his email address.

konradstrawn@gmail.com

Made in USA - Kendallville, IN
63258_9781968253400
10.07.2025 2227